Soft Courage

A true adventure fable

Tess Burrows
and Yannick Penguin

www.eye-books.com

eye books

Extraordinary Things Done by Ordinary People

The greatest danger in life is not taking the adventure.

- George Mallory -

If there's one thing I've learnt it's this; I can't avoid tough stuff and unexpected nasty happenings, but by facing these things I find treasure.

- Yannick Penguin -

Published in 2016 by Eye Books

29 Barrow Street
Much Wenlock
Shropshire
TF13 6EN
www.eye-books.com

ISBN: 978-1-78563-017-0

British Library Cataloguing in Publication Data.
A catalogue record for this book is available from the British Library.

Typeset in Garamond and Frutiger.
Yannick's signature typeface basaed on Grace McCarthy-Steed's handwriting.

Printed by CPI Group (UK) Ltd, Croydon CR0 4YY

This is a gift for my newest grandchild, soon to be born, in the hope that we, the people of earth, may leave a beautiful planet for generations to come.

CONTENTS

INTRODUCTION

Dear Reader,

You will know that there's often an important ingredient that joins things together, like the cheese in a pizza.

Once upon a time there was a passionate quest to save the earth which went through many exciting adventures across the world. And its vital ingredient just happened to be me – Yannick Penguin.

Along the way, I came to see that terrifying challenges enable me to find inner qualities that can only be described as treasures. And just between you and me, this is how I became a magnanimous superhero!

So it seemed fun for me to tell my story which, though told from a slightly curious angle, is quite true.

It's a bit like a treasure hunt,
rather like life.
This is for you …

Yannick

COURAGE

Accept the fear

It's difficult to say whether I was actually born or not, but I can remember the awakening of my mind as clearly as the cracking of an egg on a snow-capped glacier under a sparkling sun.

I was poised at the open door of an iron bird with huge wings that was soaring hundreds of metres up in the sky. Yes, I know, all sorts of species have wings, but these ones were awesomely powerful. And noisy.

I was scared stiff. I'm only small and everything around me seemed so big. Thank goodness My Human was there. She looked odd for a Mum, devoted to single-handedly bringing up three children, for she wore dungarees, heavy boots and goggles, but just being near her gave me a warm feeling that all was well.

Though I have to say that on that particular day – the day of my beginning – my fantastic, intrepid human was having a bumpy moment. Her face was dark with dread, like an overcooked fish finger.

"I'm sorry, Yannick," she said, shaking her head. "I'm finding it hard to launch us into nothingness. I know the 'chute is meant to open automatically and that all I have to do is pull the emergency chord if it doesn't open. But my brain is stuck; it won't give my body the correct instructions."

She paused, and the iron bird roared. Then she bent down and spoke directly into my ear. "I can't do this for myself, Yannick, I'm too scared. But if we look beyond the fear, at the intention behind it ... if we think of the people with mental disabilities who'll get the sponsorship money ... maybe then we can do it. For them. Those whose lives we might change."

I looked up at her, and saw strength. She was convinced that the way to act was to accept the fear and focus instead on the reason for doing it. Then ... just do it.

At the shouting of the word "Jump!" an empty space rushed up to meet us and we were floating dreamily through the air. It felt amazing. Liberating. Important.

"This shock was an awakening of your mind," My Human said later. "It's the first time you've done something for someone else."

Flippin' Flippers! She was right.

I don't remember anything before that day. Perhaps I had blotted it out subconsciously because it wasn't exciting and had little to do with character building. Ah yes – character building is what my life is all about. Which would explain why challenges like this come at me thick and fast, hitting me with "I'm not sure I can do this," yet having to find ways to keep going.

But then who am I to say. I'm only a little being, a flightless bird – a penguin.

That night, after the parachute jump, I had a dream that I would never forget.

I'm sitting on the shelf of a shop with what appears to be a handful of brothers. Certainly they all look like me – young, life-size Emperor penguins, colourful, dapper and fluffy. Though obviously not as handsome.

"I'm bored," I say to them. "Nothing ever happens around here."

"Well, our job is just to sit and look cuddly," replies the one to my left.

*"Not me. I'm going to do something with my life,"
I reply.*

*"You're just a penguin. Penguins don't do things with
their lives."*

*"This one does. I'm going to help the earth and make
a difference."*

"Where ever did you get that idea from?"

*"I heard it on the radio. There were humans discussing
about the trouble that the natural systems of the earth
are in. And when I heard that, something inside me was
jumping up and down with excitement."*

"You've got loose stuffing."

*"No, really ... and a voice inside my head was talking
to me."*

"That's just your ego. Your Pegbert."

"What's my ego?"

*"It's the part of a penguin that thinks it knows all the
answers. We call that part 'Pegbert'."*

*"Ah ... OK ... Well, my Pegbert says that I'm going to
be a great superhero. I'm going to be gallant and strong
... and be a world-famous penguin. So there!"*

*The brothers laugh so hard they nearly fall off
the shelf.*

I awoke to a beautiful day with the sun shining in through the bedroom window of My Human's little English cottage – my home. But the dream was dancing through my mind and I couldn't throw it off. It made me really upset with the brothers. In fact, the more the scene went round and round my head, the angrier I became.

I'll show them, I thought. Respect, that's what I want. Respect. I *shall* make something of myself. I *will* be a true superhero. Hadn't I already jumped out of an iron bird? That takes guts, you know. See – penguins are brave!

"We were raising money for others in need," My Human had said. "I've always wanted to do something for the world. The world has given me everything I need – a loving family, a good education, plenty to eat ... I see that as a responsibility. To give something back.

"And so, it was because of wanting to help others that we were forced to look inward. And there we found the nerve we needed to tackle the jump."

Sounded to me as though we'd struck gold. We'd discovered a hidden inner quality. It was courage, wasn't it? Surely we'd uncovered the inner quality of Courage. That's wonderful treasure.

And if that's not character building, what is? Flippin' Flippers!! I refuse to be the same as the brothers. They're stuck in sleeping minds. And they've never found treasure ...

As my anger calmed down I thought perhaps, because I'm so different from them and have an awakened mind, I really *am* special; surely the finding of this treasure proves it beyond a doubt. But what should I do with this discovery?

Could I aspire to be great and noble of character like a true Emperor penguin, endearing and admired for good qualities and considered to be a warrior of nature, shining a light in the world?

I would have to learn to use this courage.

So ... there and then, sitting on a chair in the sunlight, to the *peeyooh* calling of a buzzard circling overhead, I made a solemn promise.

I promise to build a better me.

The parachute jump had ignited a spark of adventure and I was hungry for more. But the thought of such danger was scary. How could I feel two opposing things at the same time? Having said that, I figured I'd better be particularly well behaved from now on or I wouldn't be taken anywhere.

I tried sitting on the bed at the cottage, looking cuddly – the penguin brother had said my job was to be ordinary. My Human gave me lovely big cuddles which I adored. The trouble was it seemed to bring on jealous behaviour from the other soft toys around the house. They were standoffish and rude to me.

"You're just a jumped-up ball of fluff," sneered Casey, an old and much worn bear who everyone else looked up to. "I'm the one who deserves attention around here."

"You'll never be as tough as us," said one of his gang. "You'd better not come near ... or those cute looks of yours won't be around for long."

"Why would I want to be friendly with any of you, anyway?" I said crossly. "None of you are superheroes like I am."

They seemed most interested in sitting around all day, doing nothing. Not for me. I'm not going to forget my promise. I don't want to end up like them vying to be cuddled as the top thing in life. I'm building a better me.

But it still hurt when I heard them joking amongst themselves at my expense. It made me feel sad and alone. Why didn't they know I was special? Just at that moment I didn't really want to be different; I wanted to fit in and be loved.

Then I remembered the courage treasure. Just thinking about it gave me strength, and a warm glow inside.

It would obviously take me a while to achieve calm at the cottage, but at least there were other things to think about. Exciting plans were afoot.

"C'mon, Yannick," My Human said one day, "I've a yearning to go up a mountain. We're going to learn how to climb."

Cool Fish!

She'd been staring at a picture of a mountain famous for its beauty, the Matterhorn in the Swiss Alps, which she'd skied past once. "We're going to stand on top of that," she said confidently.

Flippin' Flippers! Looks scary. But if she could feel positive about it then I could, too.

My ego Pegbert, who was making himself heard in my head, was wildly excited. Just think of the glory of conquering a mountain like that! Anyway, now that I'm the world's first flying penguin I need to undertake more missions to keep my adoring fans happy.

There didn't appear to be too many fans queuing up at the front door, but no doubt it's always best to be prepared ...

And so my climbing career began. We began by practising the basics. My Human tied an old grey shoelace around my middle – far too tightly I might add – which certainly didn't show off my figure to its full advantage. "At least you won't fall out and you'll be safe," she said. She clipped a heavy piece of metal, a karabiner, to my shoelace and with this I could be attached to her climbing harness at a moment's notice, ready for adventure.

We tried scaling hard granite rocks and soft sandstone rocks, indoor climbing walls and high hills all around England and Wales. I was positioned behind My Human and assisted in the upwards motion at tricky moments by flapping my flippers.

One of my favourite places to climb, I discovered, was on cliffs overhanging the sea, where I could sense the tang of the salt in the air and stare down at the crashing waves far below us. No doubt like my natural penguin ancestral home.

One day she said, "We're ready to climb the Matterhorn."

Cool Fish!

We travelled by train, ferry, bus and hitch-hiking lifts to the Alps. She carried a rucksack so heavy that she could barely lift it onto her back and I worried about adding to the weight and being left behind. However, I was fixed on the pack securely – horribly close to a lethal looking ice-axe – but at least I was on board.

"You'll make a wonderful pillow," she said.

My Pegbert reacted indignantly. Huh! I'm meant to be a superhero, not a pillow. Hope they don't put *that* bit in the newspapers!

Pegbert was becoming a bit annoying.

We set up our tent alongside those of My Human's local mountaineering club. The Matterhorn's almost perfect pyramid shape was an irresistible attraction, drawing in everyone who looked at it. How come mountains have magic like this?

Teaming up with a tough-looking mountaineer, we left the base hut in the darkest hour of the night. This was the way to aim for the highest point when the snow was hard and safe. Little pools of light from the head-torches shone out into the darkness, showing the way up the steep rocky ridge.

It was probably good that we couldn't see the terrifying slopes down either side as we stepped higher and higher. Before long we were having trouble finding the route as we didn't want to stay on the exposed ridge where the rocks were loose, and we became slower still when we had to travel one at a time to remain safe.

Then the weather changed. The sky seemed to close in and it started snowing. We could barely see in front of our beaks. Flippin' Flippers! Before long we were soaked.

There was no question of what we had to do. We turned back.

That was when the storm hit. Thunder rolled around and around. There was worry about lightning hitting the metal ice-axes. We made painfully slow process abseiling where we could down the east face. Heavy wet ropes. Cold fumbling fingers. Soggy flippers ...

I was happy that I could feel the inner strength of the courage treasure and knew that My Human would be accessing it, too.

But would we get down the mountain?

All of a sudden there was a loud crack and the ledge we were standing on moved. My Human swung to catch a hold with her ice-axe, reeling as it bashed her face, but just in time scrambled out of the way as – in a roar of stones and snow – our ledge disintegrated and plummeted downwards for hundreds of metres. I could feel her shaking.

But it wasn't over yet. Just in the second that it takes to hold a breath, the mountaineer gave a shout: "Watch out!" Looking up, I could see a boulder the size of death plunging straight towards us. There was no time to do anything but watch, mesmerised, as it landed right before us, then jumped over our heads and continued its awesome journey downwards.

Phew!

"There must be life's work still left to do," said My Human, relieved. "I bet there's treasure there in learning to value life ..."

It took eight hours to reach the safe snow back by the hut. We were older and perhaps a little wiser, but I certainly felt there was no treasure to be found in failure.

By the time we arrived back home a deep sense of this failure took hold of me. I felt hopeless and my ego Pegbert was annoyed.

How am I ever going to achieve great things if I can't even get up a decent mountain? I'm fed up with being ordinary. I so want to be a better me.

One of My Human's friends greeted us at the cottage. She wanted to hear all about the Matterhorn, but as soon as she laid eyes on me she started drooling. "Ahh, how sweet you are."

Grrrr, growled Pegbert. Doesn't she know I'm a superhero in the making? That I'm going to save the earth? It's very difficult being in such a small body. Size isn't everything, you know.

"Did you know prehistoric penguins that roamed the earth were the size of men?" My Human said.

Now we're talking ...

"Really?" the friend looked at me with more consideration. "So where did Yannick get his name from?"

"Well actually," My Human replied, "he was named after the French tennis player Yannick Noah, who played tennis in a fun, joyful way. So Yannick Penguin carries fun and joy with him wherever he goes."

Oooh. I guess this showed that My Human believed in me. Perhaps I ought to stop being miserable and start living up to my name by spreading fun and joy ...

But then things got bad. I was, wait for it ... placed in the washing machine. On a *hot* wash. Spun round and round with soapy suds. Penguins like water yes, but going round and round in a whirlpool, tossed all over the place ... Help! My skin might shrink! It was so undignified. I was mortified.

And Pegbert was doubly frustrated. I'm deeply wounded ... and determined to hang on to my hurt feelings.

My Human had three boys who sympathised with me. They weren't that keen on the washing bit either. Elder Boy thought baths were for sissies. Middle Boy was always in the mud playing football anyway.

And Young Boy considered it essential to hang onto any hard-won dirt.

In many ways I felt that they were my natural brothers. They were always up for great play even though it tended to get out of hand and I would end up being thrown around and left in strange places like the rubbish bin, or the cat's bed, which was particularly worrying.

That day Young Boy had an argument with a friend and was feeling hurt, too. "You can only be hurt if you choose to feel hurt," said My Human, giving him a hug. I was convinced that didn't apply to penguins.

No way am I'm going to choose not to be hurt. I expect people to treat me with respect. We penguins could die out, you know ...

It's not commonly known that penguins have a higher density of feathers than other birds. So I was delighted when the days became shorter, the sun hung lower in the sky and at last winter was upon us. Proper cold and snow time. Cool Fish!

I was taken with My Human, her boys and a gang of their spotty school friends back to the Alps to speed down mountains on skis. It was wonderful to sit perched on My Human's rucksack and enjoy the freedom of the wind in my flippers as we descended effortlessly down a white carpet as though we were flying. This did my street-cred a lot of good, particularly as we waved, whooshing wildly past the boys in a heap in the snow.

Pegbert was delighted. I can't wait to gloat to Casey and his gang when we get home.

However, the journey back wasn't as comfortable as I would have liked. We ended up having to hang around in a large departure lounge. Then, wait for it ... I was stolen by the spotty boys and had to double as a rugby ball. Why can't people bring their own rugby balls?

How would you like to be thrown around at a very rapid rebound rate? I had often heard that all beings are meant to be one family and that we should give of ourselves and all that, but I mean ... what cheek! I felt quite embarrassed to be put through this in such a public place.

I'm a very respectable Emperor penguin, admittedly still small and fluffy and not grown up and for some reason an unusual colour, but where is respect for me ... indeed, respect for the animal kingdom? What is the earth coming to?

Sometimes it feels like me against the whole wide world. Oh, Flippin' Flippers ... I'm humiliated and not sure I have the hang of this Courage thing. I know it's all supposed to be character building but I can't see how this is meant to be.

How am I ever going to be a better me?

COMPASSION

OM MANI PADME HUM

However impatient penguins are, the seasons always take their time and worries are soothed. Eventually the days become longer and warmer and the sun rises higher in the sky until summer comes. Although my natural season is winter – the colder the better – this mild weather means one thing: rock-climbing! Cool Fish!

I went with My Human and a climber friend onto the cliffs of England's Southwest coast where I was encouraged to bungee-jump into the air off a sea-stack – a tower of rocks in the ocean. Fear and exhilaration were all bundled into one amazing moment of freedom and flight.

Looking around, we had the whole place to ourselves. In fact, the isolation was an important part of the excitement. There were just sea-birds crying, and fluffy clouds playing with us ...

There was something special about the joy and thrill of movement that came with the fear of risk and the dread of danger. It created a balance that needed both parts to exist. This sent exciting energy through my body which made me feel, yes I'm really alive! This feeling of being wonderfully alive was precious. It seemed to channel my awareness further to see things beyond myself.

And yet there was something I couldn't quite put my flippers on. Something I couldn't touch in spite of these happy, satisfying feelings about the fun of all this climbing stuff. I wasn't feeling big enough about it.

If I'm going to be a better me then there has to be more to it ...

We arrived home and relaxed in a big circular chair in the centre of the cottage which My Human loved. I love circles, too. They're peaceful places. It was a perfectly normal sort of a day.

Or at least it would have been if we hadn't been particularly energised at just having been climbing on, and flying off, sea cliffs. Where the danger of climbing up rocks with waves crashing below had stirred every cell of our bodies, and raised us to listen to requests seemingly from some higher purpose.

Right out of the blue, a request came floating by. It wasn't just a day-to-day sort of wafty thought, but a monumental call to arms. One that seemed to explode in both our minds: PLEASE HELP THIS EARTH. IT IS TIME.

Aha, I pondered. OK. This is a request that can't be ignored. This is what I wanted. I'm ready! Bring it on!

My Human seemed rather startled. She had always said that her main purpose of being was motherhood. That caring for her three children was what life was all about for her, that there was no room for anything else, apart from perhaps an odd little climb here and there – or a cuddle with a penguin. Now here was this immense thought with the potential to change her life. Should she listen to it? If so, what should she do about it?

Beside her on the chair was the magazine she had been reading. "Look, Yannick," she said, "I think we're meant to be helping here. This touches my heart." The magazine's main article was about big companies that were threatening to mine on the Antarctic continent, looking for minerals and oil so that they could make money.

What short-sighted and misguided thinking some humans have! Here was the last great pristine wilderness on earth being threatened by human greed. Antarctica was my ancestral home.

My fellow penguins were at risk of losing their nesting sites, of interference on their waddling routes and of pollution of this pure environment which would upset the balance of the natural systems. This couldn't be allowed to happen. Oh, no! Not if I had anything to do with it. The Antarctic needed help.

I didn't notice then that in worrying about the penguins I was actually expressing concern and consideration for others.

As was My Human. "We have to stop the wrecking of our planet, Yannick. I think we should do a protest climb, to call attention to the plight of the Antarctic. That way a small group of people can make a big splash so that others will sit up and take notice." She meant of course people and penguins, but I let it pass, as I was so caught up in her exciting idea that we, a couple of small individuals, could do something good to make a difference for the earth.

"I know. Let's climb the Old Man of Hoy. It's in Scotland, and is Britain's tallest sea stack. We love sea stacks, don't we?"

The only problem was it happens to be an extremely difficult and dangerous climb and My Human's not that good a climber. But help was at hand. The climber friend was skilful and would join us bringing another strong friend to help.

And so the first great penguin protest climb was about to take place. A huge banner covered in pictures of Emperor penguins was prepared. Across the top was printed in large lettering: ANTARTICA IS UNDER THREAT.

Cool Fish!

My Pegbert was ecstatic. I'm so unbelievably proud of being an Emperor penguin. And it seems that Casey and his gang are finally realising how important penguins are; they're unusually quiet amongst all the busy preparations.

My Human's boys helped all they could. Elder Boy even spoke for the Antarctic in the Houses of Parliament. There was much talking and collecting of money for the campaign. Finally we set off, drove north up Britain to the furthest point of Scotland until we could go no further without getting wet and then took a little ferry to the Orkney isles.

The weather map showed a hurricane low. Mountainous seas, gale-force winds and pouring rain reflected this. I'm happy to say that penguins don't get seasick, so at least I was OK. Clinging on tight to the side of the boat amidst violent tossing and turning we had our first view of the Old Man of Hoy. It's meant to look like the figure of a man.

I couldn't see it. I just thought Oh, Flippin' Flippers – we're not going up *that*, are we? Grey and foreboding, a giant rock tower with a smidgeon of green on top rose vertically out of the ocean, like a sky-scraper that had lost its way. Wooh!

By the time we had entered the harbour, transferred to a tiny boat, carted huge piles of gear to an old stone bothy and trudged with further piles across wild, wet and treeless cliff-tops to a cave near the sea stack, we were all drenched through to the bone (well, those of us in the climbing team that had bone).

From the edge of the land we could see across to the odd little platform on the top of the stack, all that was left of a one-time promontory. It looked isolated and lost, as though no one could ever reach it.

Then we peered over the precarious route we would have to scramble down to reach the bridge of wet rocks across to the base of the stack. Here the sea pounded ferociously and spewed out foam that the strong Atlantic winds carried up and threw at us like a blizzard. We stood in awe, trying to take in the magnitude of the waiting task.

"How come the whole stack doesn't just disintegrate into the sea?" My Human shouted so as to be heard above the roar of the waves.

"It's the hard base of basalt that's holding it together," the climber shouted back. "The rest of it is soft sandstone. You'll see when we're on it. Most of it's crumbly and comes off in your hands. I don't think it'll be long before the whole thing will fall into the ocean."

Even I, as a novice, could see that this was definitely in that climbing category known as dodgy. But I was happy to take the risk because we were going to help the penguins. Our danger was nothing compared to that of thousands of penguins and their environment that was threatened now and for generations to come.

After the fiasco on the Matterhorn I had an idea that I ought to be praying to something for protection and good conditions. I'd heard My Human talking to some sort of Great Oneness. I didn't understand how this method worked, so I thought it was far easier just to have a word with the nature fairies.

Nature fairies are magical invisible elementals who hang about with penguins quite often. They work with the life force of living things. The trouble is, they tend to be rather shy around humans. But whilst the climbing team were discussing the route up, I managed to call in a couple of fairies and whisper that we were trying to save the Antarctic and it would be lovely if we could have some help from the natural systems.

By the next day the wind and most of the rain had abated and a thin sun was trying hard to shine. Wonderful. All systems go.

A gang of grey seals were watching as two men, a lady and a penguin roped up and set off up the east face of the vertical pillar. Previously, only experts had dared to take this route.

The climber went first, taking the main risk with no rope above him, carefully and skilfully finding holds for his hands and feet amongst the loose rock, flowing like a dancing spider, until he found a jutting-out bit of slab to tie onto and belay. This involved taking in the rope that My Human and I were on so that it was always taut and would hold us should we suddenly fall.

My usual place on the back of her harness was occupied by ... a tree! I suppose if I had to be usurped by something, then there could be worse things than a tree. This was a rare *notofagus antarctica* which once graced Antarctica eons ago.

She thought it would be a fine thing to plant on the top of the Old Man of Hoy to honour the present-day icy Antarctica. Though why anyone would bother to bring a tree when they had a perfectly good penguin to honour Antarctica I've no idea.

Anyway, the main problem with this tree was that it was in a plastic bag filled with soil and the bag swung from side to side as she climbed upwards. Since I was beneath it, it was bashing me on the head. Talk about uncomfortable!

When we reached the ledge where the climber was we precariously helped him pull up a large gear bag assisted by his hefty friend who pushed at appropriate places coming up behind. He himself was carrying a heavy rucksack. It was a slow and laborious process which had to be repeated over five pitches.

Some of it was traversing sideways which was very hairy. Much was slippery with spreading lichen and we also had to avoid the hazard of seagull-like birds called fulmars who insisted on vomiting in the face of anyone who came near their nests. Fulmars are not my favourite cousins. Imagine if everyone went around being sick on relatives they didn't like! Even so, I think the worst bits were the overhangs which took committed focus and frantic flipper flapping.

There was certainly no energy to look back at the mainland, or down at the wildness of the sea far below even if I'd wanted to. Though I did peep at one little piece of magic. Encouraged by odd rain showers not far away and sunshine which seemed to be supplied just for us, the dance of the natural systems produced a beautiful rainbow. Not just a normal arc – oh no – but a complete circular rainbow. How about that?

After four exhausting hours we scrambled up onto the two-tier sloping platform of grass about the size of half a tennis court, perched way up in the sky. We'd made it! The evening light was just beginning to fade. Out to sea the lights of ferries scudded by, as if our last connection with civilisation.

Across the middle of the platform was a crack in the rock giving almost enough room for us to squeeze into and settle down at awkward angles in sleeping bags for the night and hope we could keep from being too cold. The main thing was to tie ourselves onto a rope which the climber set up from one side of the platform to the other, suggesting that we had "better not sleepwalk tonight".

"I doubt if anyone has slept up here before," said My Human, struggling to find a comfortable position on the hard, damp rock using the banner as bedding and being careful to remove her contact lenses without them blowing away. Luckily, there was only a moderate breeze.

"Night-night everyone."

We lay listening to the endless wash of the waves far below and looked up at the stars which spoke to us of immensity, timelessness and beauty. As we gazed, a curtain of waving brightness swept the heavens as though joining everything together, stirring something deep within me of the fragility of our earth and its place in space. It was a time of not-knowing ... a time to wonder.

It made me feel happy that I was being useful as a comfy pillow for My Human. She snapped on a tiny light and left it on as a symbol of our vigil, keeping watch for the Antarctic.

In the morning after a breakfast of pumpernickel bread and honey, the important work began. First up was the job of unfurling the banner and hanging it over the eastern edge. The tricky bit was not letting ourselves be catapulted over as it billowed out as a sail.

Eventually we had it set so it could be read by the photographers who had gathered on the mainland. The plan was for the iconic image of penguins on the Old Man of Hoy to be sent off on the media wind around the world to influence the debate and decision makers in the Antarctic Treaty Nations.

I'm so brilliant, bragged Pegbert. Just how proud can one little penguin get!

Then we had to plant the tree. This took place on the south-western edge in a slight hollow giving it only some small shelter against wild Atlantic gales. "Be brave, little tree," My Human crooned.

Boy, was I pleased to get rid of that!

The final job was the burying of messages sent by some supporters who wanted to acknowledge that they backed our campaign, but were too busy (or some such excuse) to actually climb up the Old Man of Hoy with us. We placed the messages in a tiny tin and hid them under rocks on the top. "It's a nice way for lots of people to be part of this," said My Human, pleased with the idea.

Sorted! Now all we had to do was get down.

My Human peered over the edge. Big mistake! Long way straight down. I could see that she was scared. I'm sure she was using her courage treasure, just as I was trying to do, to overcome the terror of launching into the first abseil.

I know it's hard to believe it was necessary with all my experience of flying ... But I was still dangling on a longer shoelace even though the tree wasn't there anymore and so I rolled wildly with every movement. This wasn't helped by the next abseil which involved an enormous swing to reach the ledge. Flippin' Flippers!

I was relieved to get down and relax the focus of worrying about safety. It had been a tough mental as well as physical challenge for My Human and myself because of our inexperience. But it was all worth it. Along with the efforts of many other groups, there was a good result. The Antarctic Treaty Nations declared a fifty-year ban on mining, so the Antarctic would remain a wilderness. Conservation triumphed over consumerism. A part of our planet was saved.

Most of all, I found I was relieved for my fellow penguins. My heart space felt warm with the knowledge that they would be OK. I must have been quite concerned about them. Wooh, I guess I was genuinely more worried about others than I was about myself. How about that! That was certainly a good result. It was exciting as it gave me the realisation that all by myself I had discovered an inner quality, a treasure.

I'd found some compassion. It might not be huge amounts, but it was a start. And I knew now that to find it I just had to think about others and their needs. Then bingo, Compassion! Real treasure indeed! Cool Fish! This'll help with my character development.

What next?

No – not the washing machine. Anything but the washing machine!

FRIENDSHIP

FRIENDSHIP

Friendship for the earth: not conquering

nature but making peace with it

"**O**h, what a shame. You're all dirty. Again." Casey greeted me at the cottage with his nose in the air. One of the gang sniggered, "Here comes the penguin puddin'. I see he's even fatter than ever." "I'll soon knock the stuffing out of him!" growled another.

"Get stuffed yourselves!" I shouted back.

But there was one young member of the gang who stood up to the others. This was Footie, a brave, cheeky little black-and-white sheepdog from the Canary Islands. He had long whiskers and unruly ears, one standing upright, the other flopping over. "Ye Gods! Tell me about the climb," he yelped, and then proceeded to listen, wide-eyed.

"Well, you see, it was terribly dangerous, but I just managed to pull through ... Of course they want me there for the next one ..."

Was there to be another climb? Is it possible to create something just by thinking it so?

My Human took me to see a man with a vision who was beating a drum to stir people to do things to change the world for the better. He always wore a blue beret on his head which signified that he was working for the United Nations, showing that we can all work together to help each other. He inspired people to believe they could indeed do something as individuals.

The Visionary was delighted with the success of the climb of the Old Man of Hoy. "This is the way I want people to rise up," he said. "Climbing to high places to shine a light for the needs of our earth. The watchwords are: One World. One Family. One Nature!"

He spoke intently, blue beret askew on his head, as though there was nothing else that mattered at that particular moment except what he was passionate about. "The UN Secretary General calls it a new kind of loyalty, an earth patriotism. Not conquering the world of nature, but making peace with it."

My Human's eyes shone. How could she not be swept up in his enthusiasm?

"This is my dream. It's called Climb For The World. On UN Peace Day, we'll have people walking and climbing in their particular places everywhere across the globe, raising funds for UN environmental and humanitarian projects ...

"There will also be a grand focal climb on the Eiger, the infamous Swiss mountain which has claimed so many lives ... And representatives from every continent on earth will climb up the different faces and ridges of this mountain, coming together for a meeting at the summit. It will be harmony of nations."

It was a daring plan.

More importantly he added, "Yannick looks like a cool sort of penguin. Perhaps he would like to come and represent the Antarctic."

He'll have to have a word with my agent, of course ...

Even a small penguin such as I could see that you not only have to dream a dream, but you have to believe in it with everything you have for it to come true.

The Visionary put his heart and soul into his plan. Endless things had to be done. Endless problems had to be overcome. But it would happen. My Human joined him to help all that she could. "The dream is to give power to the people," she said.

To encourage as many people as possible to take part and climb their mountain or hill, the Visionary arranged for five hundred high points in Britain to be manned by groups of venture scouts on the day. They were going to stamp world citizen passports for those that came.

One day we were fixing a Climb For The World banner onto a tall limestone pinnacle in the Peak District where there were going to be many participants. To make the promotional photographs look family friendly, My Human's Middle Boy was allowed to climb to the top of it. A dare-devil twelve-year-old, he was obviously thrilled. Don't know why they didn't take a pram and a granny, too, while they were at it ...

My Human decided she'd rather not look as one of her baby boys posed on a vertical rock face, so she wandered up the valley to the camp and dumped all her gear, including me, whilst she went to find a drink. There were a couple of unfriendly-looking climbers hanging about looking bored.

Next thing I knew they had placed me inside My Human's blue plastic climbing helmet and I was floating down a river. It was a very pretty river with gurgling rocks and lush greenery and inviting grassy banks and even birds tweeting happily. But that wasn't uppermost in my mind as I started gaining speed and swirling around hazardously, floating away from everything that was dear to me.

I don't think I'd ever felt so lonely. Flippin' Flippers, I could end up wooshing over a waterfall and reaching the sea or worse, going down a sink-hole and disappearing forever ...

I watched with horror as a fallen tree trunk in the river loomed. I was going to hit it hard. Help! I'll either capsize or be bounced off on an unreachable trajectory ... There was sudden shouting and a lot of splashing interrupted by an abrupt jarring, then I became airborne before hitting the water again with a splatter and dragged heavily over green weeds.. At this point, I was grabbed by the strong hands of My Human, who looked decidedly wetter than usual.

I think this power to the people thing can be taken too far. What bothered me most was that the green weed all over me was very smelly. I just hoped that My Human might be too busy to notice ...

"We're going boating again, Yannick," she said one day, despite all the hectic Eiger preparations. This was to be a ferry ride with Elder Boy to a Greek island for a week's holiday. We sat on the deck. The sea was aquamarine, the waves gentle and the evening sun cast a red glow of contentment over us. We all relaxed. Even My Human, who always felt seasick on a boat.

"I'm learning about the usefulness of sitting really still" said Elder Boy, always a thinker. "I find I can listen to my inner thoughts and be in touch with answers to stuff."

"Goodie," said My Human "I'll try, too. What sort of answers?"

"Anything that's important to you ..."

"OK ... I need to know the answer to who I am."

"Nothing much, then ..."

As we sat quietly swaying with the motion of the waves I thought I'd better try, too. If my promise is to be a better me, then perhaps I need to know who I am now so I can recognise who I am when I become better.

I banned Pegbert from saying anything and let my mind be calm. Wooh! I found it surprisingly easy to listen to thoughts floating by .... I am the wind .... I am the waves ... I am the sunlight. Oh, great ... but then those thoughts weren't really much good, were they? I could do with sensible sort of answers. Ah well. It was fun trying.

Pegbert jumped back in. Listen to me. I know it all.

Pegbert, go away. But this time my Pegbert thoughts just prattled on and I lost the stillness.

My Human sat up suddenly. "Actually that was quite useful. I became at one with the waves and felt much less seasick. I'll try that again."

A couple of days later we climbed a steep hill for some fitness training. From my vantage point on the back of a little rucksack I watched as we came up to the top near a tiny white-washed chapel with lovely sundrenched views across the island. All of a sudden we were hit by a rogue strong wind. My Human was knocked flat on her back and fell on top of me, staggered up and fell flat again.

Flippin' Flippers! Not funny ... I'm squashed underneath!

Then she suddenly relaxed and became calm. "Wow," she said. "I tried becoming at one with the wind. That's great. It's the same technique I used on the boat with the waves. It's as though I'm now part of the natural systems and not fighting them any more. Now I can stand."

My ego Pegbert was none too pleased at being sat on.

Humph! I'd like some warning next time ...

Do humans also have their egos playing about in their minds like I do with my Pegbert, I wondered a few weeks later as a large team stood looking up at the North Face of the Eiger. This was the definitive mountaineering challenge which seduces and tests the egos of the toughest and most experienced of climbers. This time the Eiger was to be climbed out of respect for our living earth.

There were representatives assembled from all the continents. including a child of fourteen and a blind man. My Human, who has an Australian passport, was representing Australasia and it just so happened that she had the representative from the Antarctic with her. Also, the envoy from the Canary Islands appeared: Footie had managed to sneak in. Well, we couldn't leave out important countries, could we?

The Eiger's famous mile-high wall looked down on us and threw an avalanching rumble of rocks for good measure – bullets funnelling down the route. It is said to strike terror into any heart that sees it. Mine was no exception.

Flippin' Flippers ....

I decided I'd better quickly call in a gang of nature fairies as we might need some help, especially with the weather. "We have gathered here the hopes and dreams of the Visionary who is trying to make amends for humanity destroying so much earth." I said. "We need to shine a light for the future. Please let us ascend your mountain gently and peacefully. We would be most honoured to have the natural systems on our side."

The mountain winds remained calm. The skies held back the cold blanket of air.

The Visionary passed out pieces of the Flag of all Flags. This was a colourful collection of all the UN flags which split into seven strips – for the seven continents – to be carried up all sides of the mountain and reunited on the summit. A potent symbol of world citizenship.

Training and acclimatisation completed, the days of battle commenced. Two climbers set off up the North Face. They would certainly need courage. We all wished them well. Others took the Western Flank and the little-attempted South Ridge.

So that left the knife-edged ridge coming in from the East. Footie, the canine envoy from the Canary Islands, decided he'd like to travel with the child and his guides on their rope.

A wonderful African would lead the Australasian – My Human – and the Antarctican – little ole me!

Cool Fish!

Early on the second day we set out from the eastern hut, where a large gang had gathered sardine-like to shelter from the night cold. The air was thick with a chilling mist as we were at three thousand metres.

My Human was practising special breathing that the Visionary had taught her. This involved breathing out twice to every in-breath to release more carbon dioxide. But she confided to me, "I'm feeling so lousy

... My back is painful and I'm having trouble with a migraine in my eyes. I can hardly see. You're going to have to flap your flippers especially hard, Yannick."

Of course I would do all I could to help, I thought, calling up my compassion treasure. There was nothing more important to me than being with her and part of her special work.

The African moved with a rhythmical flow and sometimes pulled out a harmonica to play a tune which I knew would soon make My Human feel better. "We have to use proper African climbing calls," he said with a wide grin, shouting "Yo, Man!". Well, that'll surely help international relations between continents.

As the mist cleared I could see the child's rope ahead of us, one, two, three figures moving up the rocky ridge which snaked its way to a snowy summit and on into a clear blue sky. The slope fell dramatically away on either side. To the north my eyes were drawn to fields of snow clinging to the steep ramparts where cloud still hovered ominously. I hoped My Human was closely watching each step in front of us.

Before long she had to scramble steeply upwards looking for handholds. In some places it was as though she was riding on a horse, with one foot dangling into space a mile down the North Face and one foot a mile down the South.

This is scary, I thought from the back of her pack, looking for my courage treasure. I wonder how Footie's coping with the fear. Keep focusing ... Think about the wind balance in the flippers, that'll help. Someone had advised us, "If the leader falls you have to immediately jump over the other side of the ridge to balance the rope." Wise words, but I hope we don't have to test them out ...

Concentration was of the essence. But suddenly there was a shattering noise which nearly startled me out of my penguin skin. I could see My Human's knuckles gripping white, trying to maintain focus.

What was going on?

It was a chopper whirring close by with a cameraman hanging out of the door. Someone was waving and shouting, "Smile for the birdie". Flippin' Flippers, it was the BBC *Blue Peter* team, chasing the child on this backdrop of a knife-edged ridge. Thankfully, they soon moved on. But Pegbert was badly disturbing my focus.

Oh, just a minute. I hope you were able to get some good footage of the world famous penguin. I'm the celebrity here ...

After a further few hours of concentrated effort, the gradient suddenly eased. Phew! There was snow underfoot. We were on the summit. My Human burst into tears and was hugged by a kindly photographer. I think the strain she put herself through had been more than she cared to admit.

We came up to crowds of people hanging about, looking down onto drifting clouds and the green of the valley beyond. Everything had to be photographed. And it all had to take place on the small knife-edged summit ridge in the sky at almost four thousand metres, where it's not possible to make any mistakes. At least there was a rope fixed along it for us all to clip into. A little life-line.

There was a lot of flag waving, including the newly united Flag of all Flags. "Yo, Man!" I called happily to Footie amidst all the posing.

"Ye Gods! Yo, Yannick!" he called back from where he was whooping it up with the child. Nothing else needed to be said. I somehow knew that he understood exactly how I felt. There was a sense of common purpose. It was good to have Footie there.

My Human perched on the widest bit of the ridge with the African and the Visionary holding flags.

She was also given the privilege of the important reading from the UN Secretary General:

"While the power to destroy the earth is concentrated in a few hands, the power to save and strengthen it is widely dispersed ...." It was a reminder that we are all on this earth, like climbers on one climbing rope.

And the natural systems gave us magic. Looking down to where we were going to sleep – a little yellow tent precariously squashed up against a wall of snow – we could see the bright evening sunlight reflecting off a wall of cloud. There in front of it was a beautiful small circular rainbow with a figure in its centre. The figure had to be the shadow of My Human, as it was holding a penguin. This magnified shadow is a very rare phenomenon in nature. It's called a brocken-spectre.

"See, Footie," I shouted excitedly. "That's got to be a peace omen."

"Ye Gods! I sure hope you're right," he yelped back.

After darkness had fallen we sat in a line on the ridge for the summit meeting and read the peace messages that My Human had collected from those taking part. Then we snapped on little lights, waving them to draw swirls in the night, knowing that all round the globe thousands of other people were doing the same, having climbed to their high points. Lights in the darkness.

The next day, last off the mountain, the Visionary reached base camp just as a snow-storm came in. He said, "With the safe return of everyone it has been the most audacious climb ever achieved, helped in no small measure by the unprecedented three weeks of good weather.

"Thanks to all climbers and supporters here and round the world, we've raised tens of thousands of pounds for desperately needed life-line projects, from tree planting to clean water supplies, from soil conservation to helping war-torn children."

"Yo, Yannick! We did it!" cried Footie, ears flapping madly. "Let's celebrate!"

"Yo, Footie! " I replied. "We can sing the victory song. You bark and I'll do a penguin trumpet. That'll give the nature fairies something to dance to! Sadly, My Human doesn't drink, otherwise we could've had fun showering in champagne."

Nevertheless, she was thrilled by the success, saying "We've been part of the expression of the

Visionary's wonderful dream. He'd listened inwardly and made it come true. We can all emulate that."

I looked hard for treasure here. Hmm, don't know ... I felt my presence was properly honoured on the mountain, so I didn't have to fight too much to be noticed. But I'm not too sure that was character building.

Afterwards, the child was awarded the coveted *Blue Peter* badge with great ceremony on the TV. My ego Pegbert was furious. Where is my *Blue Peter* badge?

Shut up, Pegbert!

"My Pegbert's quite a nuisance," I confided to Footie. His sympathy immediately made me feel less frustrated.

That was when it hit me. I knew what the treasure was for this challenge. There was one thing that had made it extra special and left me filled up with feelings of being supported and cared about. It was having someone to talk to and share fun with. It was having Footie there. The treasure was Friendship. I'd made a friend.

He was wildly excited by it all. "Ye Gods, Yannick. This is terrific! Have we saved the world yet?"

INNER PEACE

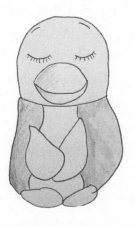

FEAR ONLY ATTRACTS THAT

WHICH IS FEARED

Back at the cottage I didn't seem to mind as much about Casey and the gang's rude comments. I think it was because Footie now believed in me. Having a friend gave me so much confidence. The others didn't want to know, but he insisted on telling them over and over again the story of the climb.

"You should have seen Yannick. He was amazing!"

I puffed up my feathers and felt smug. Pegbert beamed with pride. It made me feel good.

I also felt good because I'd been playing with My Human's boys and it just so happened that I was hiding in the rubbish bin when the time came to put the washing machine on.

Yo, Yannick!

My good mood was short lived as I overheard the telephone conversation ...

"Oh, no ... I can't believe it. How is he? ... He gave so much of himself to make the climb a success.

Everything was because of him ... of course she felt neglected ... He has such a wonderful vision, but it's cost him what is most dear..."

And then finally, "Tell him 'With love, there is no separation'."

The Visionary's wife had left him. She had taken their children and gone to the USA. My Human was very upset. I could sense the heaviness of her heart. But she knew, because she'd been through it herself, that a mother will do everything that is necessary to do what she feels is best for her children. How can life be so bittersweet?

After that, some of the sparkle left the Visionary. He missed his children dreadfully. Things began to crumble around him, but he struggled on, encouraged by the conviction that he had important work to do – to inspire others and to make a difference.

Then one day something happened that touched him deeply, something that lit his old fire ...

He phoned My Human. "Turn on the BBC news."

On TV was footage of a large sphinx-like mountain, the Sugarloaf, at the mouth of a bay overlooking a city that had golden sand beaches and calm blue water. Tongues of luscious green rainforest led up to a tall statue with arms held out in welcome.

"Many consider this the world's most beautiful city," the announcer was saying. "Rio de Janeiro, Brazil. It's here that all the world leaders are coming together for the first time to discuss the environment – the UN Earth Summit. But there is a shadow over the beauty of this carnival city. Today we have reports that the local police are cleaning up the streets in readiness for this historic conference. Street children are being shot."

My Human was too horrified to say anything.

On the phone, the Visionary continued, "We can do something about this. We can carry out a protest climb displaying a banner on the Sugarloaf Mountain for all the world to see. Then this atrocity with the street children cannot be ignored. Are you up for it?"

Was it because of the Visionary's personal pain that he had been so inspired to do something to help these children in a far-away land?

It's to My Human's credit that she did not hesitate. "Of course," was her response.

The Visionary was a good climber. I mean a seriously good climber. Think scaling the outside of the Statue of Liberty in New York or Nelson's Column in London ... You want impossible? Well, he could do impossible. So when he said let's do a protest climb on the Sugarloaf, there was no uncertainty. It could be done.

"And bring that penguin of yours," he added. "He'll be a good decoy. We'll have to smuggle a banner into the country and we need to look normal."

Anyone carrying an adorable, fluffy penguin would look normal and couldn't possibly be threatening national security. It was obvious ...

But I immediately went into a dither, a real Yannick panic.

I wish I was calmer and didn't get so stressed about things. I should try that sitting still thing ... But then, life's full of such exciting happenings. It's enough to stir anybody's feathers.

Preparations for Rio exploded into action. Cool Fish frenzy! We had both the street children and the environment to think about.

My Human collected messages written on paper leaves from British children – 'pledges for the planet' – to carry to the Earth Summit, where there was a special tree to display messages like these from children all over the world.

Middle Boy was chosen to represent Britain and send a special letter to a child in Brazil. He wrote:

... Our planet needs help. The greed of mankind has destroyed its natural balance, with corruption of nature, pollution, erosion, famine and extreme poverty taking their toll ...

... Please can your voice in Brazil represent the children of the earth. Let us bid for a healthy environment where all nature including man is at one with the planet ..."

Surely the world would listen to the simple but profound voices of the children.

But would the world listen to the message of a protest climb?

The Visionary made a gigantic banner which read CLIMB FOR THE EARTH in green and HELP STREET CHILDREN TO LIVE in red. Then he found a special suitcase with a false bottom.

Footie was devastated not to be coming with us. But he was a little dog with a big heart. "Ye Gods! Go well, my friend. We'll be thinking of you and watching out on the TV." I felt sad to be leaving him.

Even Casey muttered "Yo, man!", which sounded slightly friendlier than before, and I thought perhaps he might be more open to chatting. But then he added, "You'll never do it!" and half the gang laughed. Fortunately, there was the journey to concentrate on.

I felt distinctly nervous as we flew on the iron bird into the great city of Rio and looked down on the West Face of the Sugarloaf. The mountain is four hundred metres tall, higher than the tallest building in London, and seemingly vertical. Yes, it was perfect for displaying a message on. Many thousands of people from across the world were gathering here alongside the leaders, trying to make changes to help the environment. Everybody would be able to see it.

The Visionary wasn't wearing his beret and My Human was dressed in a pretty skirt, something I'd never seen before. Strange, this "normal" thing. She had an unusually nonchalant look on her face as we came into passport control. I could feel her clutching me rather tightly as the official stared over a pair of black-framed glasses.

"Purpose of visit?"

"Holiday," she answered, looking down and stroking me.

"Does he have a visa?" the official asked, nodding at me.

Oh, help.

The official was joking. A broad smile spread over his face and this normal family was ushered through into Rio de Janeiro.

Phew! So far so good.

We were met by a local conservationist who was very supportive of what we were doing and taken back to his flat for the night. I think he was pleased to have us to talk to. He was grief-stricken. One of his friends had just been murdered, shot as he filled up his bike at a petrol station. It seemed that he had been in the way of a petty thief.

If I ran the world, I wouldn't let humans have guns. Well, penguins don't have guns, do they?

It was barely light the next morning when we were taken, with as little fuss as possible, across the city and round along a trail through a small rainforest to be dropped off at the base of the Sugarloaf.

Now we could see the challenge ahead. The huge vertical monolith of granite and quartz towered above us, grey-beige coloured, but with an almost pink hue to it. I felt excited and scared at the same time. Flippin' Flippers! There would be no room for error here with our climb, but what worried me more was our exposure on the face. We'll be so vulnerable if someone doesn't like what we're doing ...

My Human sat with her back close against the mountain and her eyes shut. "I'm just tuning in with the Sugarloaf," she said. "Asking permission from the rock itself for us to climb. Our intention is to help the earth and its children, so we really need to be in harmony. Seems the right thing to do."

Ah, I could see quite a few nature fairies dancing with delight at this ...

"The rock feels warm," she continued. "It's as though we've been welcomed with a hug."

A little snake sunbathed nearby in the already warm sun, and darting lizards chased brightly coloured insects amongst ants rushing to and fro.

"We need to get going," said the Visionary, looking around furtively. He was ready in his harness and running the ropes through his hands. "We need to fix both the banner and the camp today."

A couple of local climbers appeared as if from nowhere to help. It was welcome and strong support; I understood the value of friendship now. Within a few hours the four corners of the banner were fixed on ropes via climbing gear to small cracks in the rock.

There was much fiddling about to get it straight and not drooping.

Also, it was a bit convex with the lay of the rock. But finally our message was displayed – fifty or so metres up in the air. Everyone in the city and via the world media would be able to read it.

Our helpers disappeared as quietly as they had come. We were on our own.

Now for the camp. The Visionary climbed up first to secure some fixing spots. Then he hoisted up the two large, red haul bags containing all our gear, using pulleys through which the ropes could run. They were made of tough heavy plastic, so hopefully would survive the bashing they received on the way up.

Then My Human and I followed and hung nearby. "I really miss not being able to put my feet on anything," she said, having to take her full weight on her harness.

"Don't worry, you'll soon get used to it," grinned the Visionary. "It takes a little while to trust the system. Just remember one rule. Always be clipped into two points." He, at least, was in his element. My Human was holding tight to everything she could that she thought was fixed and trying not to look at the drop straight down. "Mmm, trust the system," she repeated trying to smile but looking nervous.

I often hang on her harness with nothing to put my feet on. What's the big fuss about?

There was plenty to do to distract an uneasy mind. First, the two portaledges had to be unpacked and put together. A portaledge is fun. I'd never seen one before. Think hammock without the holes, a lightweight stretcher with a tape at each corner.

The idea is to try and attach the tapes to the rock in such a way as to be reasonably horizontal. Then tame it before the wind flies it around by slipping your weight on it. Then lay a sleeping bag out. Hang up everything that might be needed. And so you have a sky-bed, complete with excellent air-conditioning.

The whole process had to be carried out, of course, without dropping anything. Hmm ... fat chance of that happening. But so long as important things like penguins are tied on ...

The light of the day ended suddenly with a red blaze, a reminder that this was the tropics. We could smell the damp of the forest, hear cicadas strumming and sense bats flitting around. Our little camp settled down for the night.

"Beds are going to be a bit boring after this," My Human giggled. "Though it's not that comfy trying to sleep in a harness. At least I have my penguin pillow with me."

Ah, how that warms my heart.

The breeze was gently rocking the portaledges. There was a certain sense of airiness, particularly with the view of thousands of stars above as though we were suspended in space with them. But it was by no means dark. We looked across and down at the lights of the city which still vibrated with movement and colour. The muffled sounds of vehicles and sirens reached us.

And then there were gun shots. Flippin' Flippers! Is that yet another child whose body will be found like discarded vermin on a beach in a cardboard box?

"Night night. Sleep well!"

The next morning the vultures came. Gangs of them circled silently overhead, black wings held rigid, wrinkled heads staring down with beady eyes and hooked beaks. They made me extremely uncomfortable. Were they looking for carrion or live prey? Hopefully not fat penguin fast-food.

"I hear vultures poo on their own legs to keep themselves cool," said My Human.

This interesting fact made me feel less intimidated.

I'm glad penguins are naturally cool.

Camp breakfast was the same as dinner the night before. In fact, it was the same for every meal – oats, milk powder, dried apple rings, dates and seeds, all mixed up with water.

We were hauling one large plastic water container and two squashy water bags for the needs of the day. But the Visionary warned, "We must be extremely frugal with the water. The local climbers have said they will resupply us every three days, but we can't be sure. Anyway, let's move the camp before the day gets too hot."

Being a poet at heart he gave each camp a lovely name. The new one was called "Ear of the Wind". This was the night when the wind rose to near gale force level. We were buffeted about like a ship in a storm with the sails of our banner calling loudly above us. We worried that it might rip. Or rather, the others worried the banner might rip. I worried about

My Human being seasick on me. Happily, CLIMB FOR THE EARTH; HELP STREET CHILDREN TO LIVE held firm.

In the middle of that already scary night there were dark shapes to the south stealthily climbing up an old rusty cable. "Probably Brazilian commandos on a training exercise," the Visionary remarked. "More like police come to tear down our banner," said My Human, holding her breath in fright. "They've got us under surveillance anyway ..." I was really anxious until they'd passed us by, though I wasn't sure anyone had actually been there at all.

By the time we established camp "Eye of the Sun", there were odd plants – waxy bromeliads clinging to existence on the rock face like us – taking the hard but beautiful path, asking for hope and caring. "I feel such a lovely connection with the preciousness of life," My Human said. "I'm more relaxed, though of course still mindful of the big drop below us, but I'm used to the hanging about and the trusting now."

She seemed to be enjoying herself. There was a little nook in the rock big enough to put some gear in and she was delighted to find it sparkling with quartz crystals. She hung flags from the portaledges. And the banner was spreading its wings just below. "I feel at home," she smiled. Relaxing is catching. I got it, too. I could sense a beautiful place in my mind, full of penguins ... and fish ... and snow ...

Change came, brought by the wind. Wham! It suddenly moved to the south. That meant rain. A mad scramble took place to try out the waterproof top for one of the portaledges. But everything got wet anyway. Good thing we're not in the snow after all.

About two thirds of the way up the mountain we came to the wonderful camp "Garden of the Mists".

Though it was rather more misty than we would have liked, it was a ledge on which vegetation lived!. Small shrubs and green grasses. Butterflies dancing. Rustling even revealed a big fat rat. How did he get there? Must have been dropped by one of the vultures which still reeled threateningly overhead.

That evening we had visitors. Local climbers resupplied us with water. They also produced a special treat out of a small rucksack coolbox – snack biscuits and cold beer! The Visionary was ecstatic. But, oh Flippin' Flippers! Whatever you do, don't give My Human alcohol!

Too late. She was thirsty.

I could tell she wasn't entirely in control. It wasn't just the giggling and the casual way she took out her contact lenses and brushed her teeth unlike the usual careful routine. She seemed to have lost the watchfulness that was so essential to life on a vertical rock face four hundred metres above the ground.

"Can't get this portaledge to sit correctly," she said, yanking it with both arms.

Wham! The portaledge wacked vertical against the rock, acting like a catapult.

Thud! The contents of the portaledge fell onto the tiny holding of grasses which had been so liquid green in the sunlight.

Slish!

Silence.

Then a very small voice: "I think I've dropped my contact lenses down the mountain."

The Visionary peered over the edge of his portaledge. "Are you tied on?"

"Everything's so hazy. I'm almost blind without my lenses. I can't possibly climb further."

"Are you tied on?" he insisted.

"I'm sorry ..." she said in an even smaller voice and tied herself on. "I've let you down."

"Well, not much we can do tonight. We'll have a look in the morning."

"It was my orange wash-bag that went. They were inside, along with my spare pair of lenses." She was close to tears now. "But that's not all. It's worse. There were papers – the bundle of messages from the children ..."

I knew she would think this the worst crime of all. I'd never seen her look so wretched, so utterly dejected.

But superhero Yannick was there.

Sometimes, Dear Reader, when life hits you with nasty stuff, you just need a penguin to cuddle. It helps, I'm telling you. It's got something to do with compassion for yourself.

"I'm so sorry I've put you at risk," she said to the Visionary as he prepared to abseil down into the rainforest to search for her belongings.

It had rained in the night, adding to her misery, but

the dawn had brought the promise of drying out, and a sunny day.

"Don't hold out much hope of finding anything," he said, leaning back to put his weight on the rope and took a couple of steps backwards, waving with his free arm as he went.

That was when the whirring came.

Wrrrm! It was the sound of rushing.

It all happened so quickly.

What!?!

Something from above.

Three very large lumps of concrete passed by.

A burst of dust just to the left of the Visionary.

Flippin' Flippers! Dangerous or what!

My Human instinctively dived inwards for the slight cover of the mountain and clutched the lifeline of the safety slings. But it was the Visionary who was exposed and at risk out on the rock. After a moment all was quiet except for wildly beating hearts. He searched the summit and skyline. That sort of thing doesn't happen by accident. Was someone trying to stop us? The police most likely.

He had no choice but to keep on going down.

My Human and I waited anxiously for his return. "You know, Yannick, miracles do happen," she said.

"You just have to expect them."

I tried expecting a delivery of flying fish, but nothing seemed to happen. Perhaps I got the technique wrong.

It was well into the afternoon when a smiling face appeared. He had risked parts of the old cable to ascend. "Well, here you are. One soggy orange wash-bag, intact! Took a bit of searching for in the rainforest. And I had quite a job retrieving the children's messages. They were scattered over a wide area with some up in the trees, but I think I found most of them."

She was right. Miracles do happen. Visibly emotional, she gratefully accepted both the rather worse-for-wear messages and the gift of the return of her sight.

The climb could continue.

But the day had been lost and the following evening found us struggling, running out of light and with no holds on the rocks. I was feeling quite stressed by the whole situation. After an intense climb that lasted seemingly for hours, we ended up clinging to a belay point with the Visionary.

"Thank you, Sugarloaf," My Human said, stunned and elated. "We're part of you and you're taking care of us."

Oy! Don't forget all the help there from flapping flippers!

But where were we going to sleep?

There was a short pitch to a stance, more hauling of gear and then the most wonderful thing. "You're going to like this," said the Visionary. The mountain had provided for us in our hour of need ... it produced a cave, a magical cave.

The cave was full of nature fairies, dancing.

I felt as though a big wave had come and washed all my anxiety away.

"I love it here," said My Human. "I don't want to reach the top and have to face people. I'd rather just stay here in this beautiful cave. I feel so much in harmony with the Sugarloaf and all its moods."

"And with each other," said the Visionary.

I had to admit I could stay in this cave forever, too. All the problems of risk and worry had disappeared and I was left with something I had never experienced before. Calm! A deep sense that I could accept whatever happens around me, even if the mountain fell down ... Wow! What was this?

Could it be treasure? What's it called? Then I realised ... I remembered ... My Human was often saying that the way to world peace is by individuals finding inner peace. That if we can find our own inner peace then we're making a difference in the world. That must be what I'm feeling. Peace inside me.

Cool Fish! That's the treasure – Inner Peace.

I felt really pleased that I'd worked it out. Then I realised that it was OK to experience inner peace now that the stress had been taken away but ... a big but ... what about finding it when life was throwing nasty stuff at me? Now that would be a test.

At least now I've experienced it I know what I'm looking for. So hopefully it'll be easier to find in the future.

Anyway, Pegbert has other ideas ...

C'mon, let's get ready to be in the news; there's world-wide coverage out there. Time to party!

Right. Life cannot stand still.

The next morning we climbed up to the summit to be welcomed with great cheering by the large crowd which had taken the easier route – the cable car.

There were warm messages of support and congratulating speeches by all sorts of VIPs.

One said, "Your action has made the horror of what's happening to the street children become an international issue. It cannot be ignored now."

Another said, "This brave climb shows us that a few determined individuals standing up for what they believe can make a difference and help change the world."

My Pegbert was unbelievably proud. This is what I always wanted. And so many photographers and journalists from around the world clamouring for interviews …

The Visionary declared, "In our love as parents we were moved to suffer the trials of living on the mountain for the eleven days of the conference, expressing concern for the children of the earth. They are our future. And for them, if not for ourselves, we need to care for the environment. Who's responsible? Every one of us. You and you and me …"

"Can we live in balance with our environment?" asked one of the journalists.

My Human responded, "We have been looking down on Rio, with its problems of richness and extreme poverty, both of the environment and of the people. As here, so in the wider world. We believe if we listen to the children, then there is hope."

Back in Rio, we were celebrities. We were interviewed in a TV studio to speak for the protection of the unique rainforest at the Sugarloaf base, happily resulting in a new park.

We went to meet the street children, the lucky ones who were safe at the refuge where our sponsorship money would go (along with some for the threatened Amazon flooded forest). And most importantly, we delivered the well-travelled children's messages to the special tree.

The Earth Summit – billed as "the most important meeting the world has ever known" – drew to a close. One twelve-year-old girl bravely stood up in front of the world's delegates challenging them with "... I'm only a child, but here in Brazil, one child living on the streets told me 'I wish I was rich and if I were I would give all the street children food, clothes, medicine, shelter, love and affection.' If a child on the streets who has nothing is willing to share, why are we who have everything still so greedy?"

Hmm ...

This made the Visionary miss his children even more. He made plans to move to the USA to be near them. We would miss him.

It got me thinking about my promise. In spite of all the success I still feel I have a long way to go to build a better me.

HUMILITY

Every positive thought makes for a

better world

I was wildly excited about being back at the cottage again with My Human's boys and Footie. That was, until I got caught by the washing machine.

I'm sending a report to the Royal Society for Penguin Chick Atrocities.

Footie wanted to hear all about the protest climb. "Ye Gods," he exclaimed, "we thought you'd end up in gaol!"

Casey was grumbling from the sofa, "You're not the only being on the planet you know ..." But I ignored him and boasted "Flippin' Flippers, I was too clever for that ... though the vultures nearly got me. And the street children at the refuge wanted me to stay with them, but of course I couldn't bear to be separated from My Human. Besides, I wouldn't want to miss out on the next adventure."

"You mean we still haven't saved the world? Let's get on with it. Lead the way ..." Footie's ears flapped about enthusiastically like flippers in a snowstorm and I thought how lucky I was to have such a supportive friend.

It seemed that My Human was of the same opinion (about the world, not the ears). So spurred on by the knowledge that it was possible for individuals and small groups to make a difference she thought she'd give the youngsters some activist training.

She gathered Young Boy and one of his sporty friends (I'd got it wrong before – they were sporty, not spotty, friends), plus myself and a delighted Footie and informed us we were going to do a vigil for the earth in the apple tree in the garden. That sounded a bit pathetic to me. I mean, you can only fall two metres. Where's the excitement in that?

It involved quite a tricky heave to get up into the tree and onto three old planks which served as a ledge. And by the time we hoisted up all we would need for the night we felt quite pleased with our camp. I guess life is about the intention behind what you do, not about how far you can fall.

Firstly though it was important to do the campaigning bit. We jumped down and walked to the local pub to collect some funds for the Amazon project. I would've preferred a "disadvantaged penguins" project, but we did quite well. And then we returned to the tree for the night.

It wasn't the best cooked dinner. We set fire to the tree twice in the process and most of it was donated to the deer. But we snapped on a little light and spoke good wishes for the earth, feeling strongly that every positive thought makes for a better world.

My Human made sure we were all tied on to the branches and we hunkered down to sleep, pretending we were a mile up and the owl noises were actually ghosts of dead adventurers. The pillows fell out and then the water bottles and then Young Boy, who was hoisted back in without even waking up. The summer dawn came early, with gangs of birds shouting, so the boys climbed down to play in the garden. The rest of us settled into a Sunday morning lie-in.

"Ye Gods! What's the treasure to be learned here?" asked Footie.

"No idea," I replied. "But the children show us that even simple adventures can be fun."

Human children are good at seeing not only adventures but big important things in a way that avoids all the complications that adults invent. The power of the voice of the twelve-year-old child who spoke at Rio still reverberated around the world:

"It is your responsibility to look after our future for us. Please look after our earth."

Young Boy wanted to be part of it and do something. He'd been touched by the ancient wisdom of the whales and in particular, a children's global crusade that was concerned about an orca whale being held in captivity. He wanted to raise funds for this project.

Whilst it was good that he wanted to help animals, what bothered me at a fundamental level was the fact that orcas eat penguins. They're also known as killer whales. That says it all, doesn't it?

They don't casually eat them – they cleverly plot and carry out deeds like tipping up penguin-full ice-floes into waiting orca mouths. Just the thought of it had me quaking in my boots (actually, penguins don't really need boots as we can conveniently control the temperature in our feet, but if I had boots my feet would be quaking inside them).

The question was, could I use my compassion treasure found on the Old Man of Hoy to extend it to species other than penguins – in particular the orca? Now here was a test.

I talked to Footie about it.

"P'raps you could think of the orcas having to feed their babies," he suggested. But that didn't help. They were different from me and even with all this talk about all species being one family, I couldn't find any nice thoughts to think about them. I mean, how would you feel if your neighbours decided they'd like to eat you for dinner?

So I listened apprehensively to the idea that was brewing at the cottage. My Human and Young Boy would set off on bicycles, something nice and safe at ground level, on a journey to collect pledges from people to not use their cars for a number of miles. This would help them appreciate that their cars were shoving out carbon dioxide which was wrecking the atmosphere and contributing to global worming. (Yo, worms!)

Every little bit less travelled by car would help. The fact that a child of thirteen was able to bike a reasonable distance would show that it was possible to do at least something. And as a result, sponsorship funds that would go towards the whales could be raised.

So what was a reasonable distance?

"Well," said My Human, "I've never really been on a bike, but if someone can lend me one and I can get the hang of it then I think we could do something worthwhile. How about the length of Great Britain: John O'Groats to Land's End? It's a thousand miles or so."

Young Boy was all for it. I'm sure it had nothing to do with the fact that he would need to miss school for a month.

Elder Boy kindly lent My Human his bike and showed her how it worked.

Of course it was unthinkable for them to go adventuring without their superhero penguin. They would take me.

But my ego Pegbert was doing some serious plotting ... Hmm, how can I scupper the orca plans along the way? Saving the world is the important thing, but a world without orcas would be a big improvement. Any thoughts of compassion went out the window.

There might be one way ...

In the meantime there were weeks of hard work in order to gather gear, collect pledges, campaign and raise funds. Young Boy was given a smart blue bike. I was given a new shoelace harness in dashing orange.

The headmaster and all the children at Young Boy's school made their own pledges and gave us a rousing send-off.

The two bikes were packed to the hilt with gear, almost too heavy to push. Each one had four panniers and two racks and was decked out with signs saying JOHN O'GROATS TO LAND'S END and USE LEGS NOT PETROL.

There was just about enough room for a penguin to sit on My Human's bike. I tried various positions and opted for the bowsprit version on the front, head-on into the wind. From here I could direct proceedings and help manoeuvre turns by flapping flippers.

Waving goodbye to a forlorn little Footie, we took the train to the northeast of Scotland and managed to get the bikes on a bus to John O'Groats, which lived up to its name of seeming like the end of the world. Here we lined up in front of a white mark in the road. This was it. The right date: it was World Environment Day. We were cycling for the earth!

I knew what I had to do. Actually, it was more what not to do. On previous adventures I had got into the habit of talking to the nature fairies. They had been very good at communicating with the natural systems, in particular to help with the weather. It was a win-win situation to save the earth. It seemed that nature fairies would only assist if asked. No doubt it was natural law.

So my cunning plan this time would be to *not* ask them for help. That way we would in all likelihood be battling horrendous weather, especially the wind. Young Boy being only a child would find it too tough and give up. I mean, children don't set off to bike a thousand miles, do they? It just doesn't happen. So the whole expedition would have to be abandoned, and none of the sponsors would pay up for the orcas.

I felt quite proud of my plot.

The first day we managed five miles. I have to say My Human was pathetic. She was scared of biking anywhere near traffic; she kept stopping to adjust things and was dreadfully slow. Poor Young Boy kept looking at his speedometer in despair. After helping put up the tent in a campsite, he went off to find friends his own age to enjoy an evening on the town.

Can't say I blame him.

I think that was the last time he had any spare energy. The next day the wind had built up from the west. It grew steadily as we headed westwards along the wild Atlantic coast with brief glimpses of seals and puffins. And the road wound uphill and downhill and – then, always – uphill again.

The wind was dead against us, seemingly blowing us backwards. It blew day after day as we turned south across wild bog-land, and still it seemed to blow straight into us. It just blew and blew and blew. My flippers were no match for the wind. They felt like they were permanently forced backwards as though I were a champion ski jumper.

There was much groaning and grunting of bodies not wanting to tackle this challenge. "I really don't want to do this," shouted My Human. "I wish I was at home in bed."

"What are we doing here anyway?" Young Boy shouted back, angry tears on his cheeks, stolen hastily by the wind. "I had no idea it would be torture like this. I miss my friends. I miss my pussy cats. I want to give up!"

Ah. Pegbert perked up. So soon?

We stopped by the side of the road, letting the bikes fall, with me prickled in the rough heather.

High curlews called overhead .There was nothing but rolling peat-land to the distant horizon where snow-capped mountains waited. Nothing to stop the wind.

My Human dug out some bananas, bread and a tube of yeast pate known as semtex. "C'mon. This'll make us feel better. We can do this. I'm going to practise being one with the wind. I'm sure it'll help. And think about all the people whose pledges we're carrying. We've told them it *is* possible to use legs, not petrol. There's no turning back. No giving up. Let's keep trying."

Young Boy revived somewhat with food. "Yes, and I'm going to think of the orca whales that we're helping. That'll keep me going."

But to move was to pile pain on top of aching muscles crying out to stop. And the wind kept blowing straight at us. That night we collapsed in an exhausted stupor by the side of the road and threw the tent up, even though we were in a peat bog. No one had the energy to light the stove for a hot drink. That was when the rain started and the level of water rose and I worried that the tent might float away.

That thought seemed to drive everyone to get up at first light and squash soggy wet gear into the panniers and keep going, mind carrying body. I still travelled on the front rack, wet and muddy, but free. To adventure is to have freedom – the freedom of not knowing what's going to happen next.

By the time we had skirted the harshness of the highlands and come steeply down to long, beautiful Loch Ness, famous for its monster, the muscles of the bodies were more at ease and had developed some fitness. Of course we looked for monsters, but only found those of the mind.

My Human had sorted out a monster-killing technique, the one that helped her the most. "The important thing is to visualise where we're going," she shouted to Young Boy. "Visualise us safe and well each day. See the picture with your inner eye – safe and well at Land's End. It'll inform our minds what is to happen and keep at bay all those drifting negative thoughts."

"I'll do that every day," he shouted back, starting to feel happier. There was a good chance here in this tourist area that we would find a chip shop. He'd discovered there were few more important things in life. "I'll visualise chip shops for us!"

I felt so proud of Young Boy for what he was achieving. That was when it hit me. Flippin' Flippers – what had I been doing trying to scupper things? I saw the incredible effort that he was putting in, knowing he was helping the orca whale. He'd been finding the courage treasure, the same one I'd discovered on the parachute jump.

I'd seen him many times dead beat, collapsed on the side of the road crying angry tears at Great Oneness for giving him more than he could cope with. And yet, even when things seemed physically impossible, he always found a way to dig deep for that inner strength he needed to keep going.

Suddenly I felt ashamed of my behaviour. He was my brother. His loving support was important to me. I'd let him down. I needed to say sorry.

But Pegbert insisted otherwise:

I'm right. Down with orcas!

Shut up, Pegbert. When I'm planning nasty things I don't feel good about myself. In fact, I feel like I'm hurting myself more than the orcas.

Perhaps Casey was right; I'd been arrogant and self-centred, though I didn't want to admit it. Something about that acknowledgement made me feel a little easier with myself.

But I still couldn't feel compassion for the orcas. So I reckoned the next best thing was just to not think of them at all. My way of apologising would be to help Young Boy visualise chip shops. I immediately felt lighter inside.

Soon a shop appeared and we sat down in front of a plate of hot chips. Gold dust! The owner wouldn't let us pay, and we were touched by his kindness. Not only his, but that of so many people we met who wanted to help us, offering us all sorts of interesting things like goat's milk and talking parrots ... as well as pledges and sponsorship.

"It feels like the way is strewn with angels," said My Human.

Actually when my flippers are bent back I sort of look angel-like.

And for sure I feel more angel-like. Well, shall we say less arrogant and grumpy, when I use the monster-killing technique of visualising us all safe and well. It makes me feel more positive, which somehow keeps Pegbert quieter.

The effort continued. By now our longest day mileage had reached to almost forty. But then we had an agonising climb up into the Grampian Mountains at Glen Coe, the site where a great battle had once taken place. Here, in a snowy cold blizzard a lone piper in a kilt stood playing the bagpipes. It was unexpected – stirring and mournful. This is obviously how the Scots get their toughness.

Wonder how I'd look in a kilt?

We hit the city of Glasgow, somewhere we'd wanted to avoid, on a Sunday afternoon with as little traffic as possible, but My Human was still terrified. Thank goodness I was there beside her to give moral strength. Then onwards south to achieve our best day-mileage by far – sixty!

This was helped by the fact that we knew we had to reach a school in Dumfriesshire which had invited us to talk to the children. But it did not help that we arrived too shattered to speak.

The rain poured relentlessly as we entered England. But we had to push on south, resenting the effort we needed to exert on the hills of the Yorkshire Dales instead of eyeing their loveliness, as we had a date in Manchester.

Here, where we noticed the pollution affected our breathing, Young Boy spoke at the Alternative

Transport Rally and won first prize for his inspirational method of getting there. The boy who won second prize came in a wheelie-bin. Pity there wasn't a penguin category for wind-powered wheelie-bins. I might have done well there. Or for waddling. D'you know Emperors have to waddle up to seventy miles across the ice?

We were pleased to leave the city and move ever onwards south along the Welsh border, green and beautiful though no less strenuous, through the ancient forest of Dean and the mysterious Wye valley, crossing the swaying Severn Bridge to speak at a school in yet another city, Bristol.

The teacher wanted us to encourage the children to think about what they were doing to the environment. But they were so excited to see me that I was over-cuddled and passed from child to child until a fight broke out. I became flustered custard and went into a Yannick panic, worrying that I might be separated from My Human. Where's all this inner peace when I need it? I was rescued just in time and taken to the nice, safe newspaper and radio people. It's not always easy being famous.

Heading into the Southwest, we managed to get lost. Finding a good route was always tricky as the quick big roads were far too scary and the small wiggly ones tended to have lots of hills – mind you, Devon was all hills anyway.

We'd stop and consult the map in lovely gentle farmland with inquisitive cows peering wide-eyed at us over hedges, wondering what all the hurry was about. I think I like cows. I feel quite safe around them. And presumably they feel safe around me. Penguins aren't likely to slit their throats and eat them.

As we came closer and closer to the end, Young Boy concentrated on beating his record readings from his speedometer. One day downhill with a following wind he achieved perfect speed – that state which young humans are so good at – being totally happy in the present moment.

Yo, Dude!

We could smell the tang of the sea air at Land's End even before reaching it on a showery windswept evening – grey and cold. No one around. Tourist places closed. Greeted by the cry of the seagulls. The lighthouse standing out to sea solid on the rocks. This was the picture we'd been visualising for so long, the one that had kept us going. But in our mind's eye there was actually considerably more sunshine, not to mention chip shops. We had to work on that technique a bit more.

We'd cycled over a thousand miles in a month and shown that it is possible to get around with pedal power rather than earth-polluting cars. And that even a child could achieve this. We'd collected tens of thousands of miles of pledges from people promising they would not drive their car.

It had been about long, tiring days, ups and downs, frustrations and joys, wet and dry, heat and cold, gales and more and more wind, through towns and far from civilisation, camp washing blown away or covered with birds' muck ... and always wondering where the next meal might come from.

The only bike problem we'd had was a rack which fell off. My Human fixed it with a safety pin; she's not highly technical. Thank goodness we never had to change a puncture.

She said, "I've been trusting that our needs will be met ... believing. Finding that still, calm place in my heart which says 'all is well'."

Young Boy said, "We wouldn't have made it without the support of each other. But it's all been worth it to help the orca whale. And I think I'm the youngest person ever to bike from John O'Groats to Land's End. Cool!"

I bet I was the first penguin to do it, too. Yo, Yannick! I had achieved another world record!

But somehow that thought didn't seem as fulfilling as before. My superior attitude that I'd been using with Casey and the gang didn't make me feel so good now. What was changing? Had I been wrong in my attitude? Certainly somewhere along the way on this adventure I'd lost some of that feeling of being so high and mighty.

There has to be treasure in this. What is it? It's humility. Cool Fish! I've found the treasure of Humility. Well, a little bit anyway ... a tiny bit ...

I was going to need it.

DETERMINATION

THE TREASURE IS IN HOW YOU PICK YOURSELF

UP AND START AGAIN

I'm sure I can find a way to sabotage the washing machine ...

I'd come home to another battle with my Pegbert. Just when I thought I was getting somewhere.

Back and forth the conversation went:

Pegbert, I have to accept what life gives me and try not to fight against things. At least that way I won't get so upset.

But my needs are not being respected. I'm being pushed around!

Isn't it more important that everyone is happy?

None of this made any difference. I still had to suffer the indignity of the washing machine. And I worried that it was causing bald patches on my head and losing some of the brightness of my colours. Most embarrassing.

In addition to Pegbert, what was even more disturbing was that I knew I had to face Casey and tell him that maybe he had been right about me all along. I couldn't do it, though. So I just ignored him and things became worse between us.

Thank goodness for my loyal friend Footie, always cheery and supportive. There should be more Footies in the world.

The following months fell into a sort of happy penguinness. Footie and I would chat for hours trying to sort out how the world worked. My Human would give me lovely cuddles. And I'd enjoy playing games with her boys when they were there. But I was still haunted by my promise. I needed to build a better me. There was a longing deep inside me for this.

I knew that I'd been lucky enough to go through challenges that had helped my character development, but I didn't want to wait around for negative challenges to happen. Flippin' Flippers! I might end up with all sorts of health problems, like being overweight or having a skin condition or being big-headed ... To my way of thinking it was far better to go out and find some adventures and grow through them instead.

So I was pleased when My Human decided that we were going climbing in the Alps again. Just a nice, happy time messing around on skis with friends.

How wrong could I have been? Our whole settled way of life was about to change.

My Human acquired herself a boyfriend, a knight in shining armour. Well, a knight in a peaked cap at least. I've no idea why so many humans feel the need to keep their brains warm ...

This was a big disaster to my way of thinking, in spite of him being good-looking, dynamic and so kind that nothing was ever too much trouble. I couldn't warm to him because I was jealous. Well, he kept spending loads of time with My Human and she'd forget about me. That's enough to make anyone jealous, isn't it?

The day the Boyfriend came to pick us up in his car is etched on my mind for ever. It was packed to the roof with adventuring equipment, barely leaving space for us. Hanging from the rear-view mirror by a red-and-yellow string was a little being. She had a graceful body, a long beak and large, pretty eyes. Her colours were not dissimilar to mine. Who was she?

"Ah, Yannick," he said. "I've brought a girlfriend for you. This is Oiseau. She's a beautiful little bird."

Joke!

You cannot be serious! You don't think I'm going to be interested in a duck, do you! Or even for that matter, be a little bit friendly. She's taken my place.

That's where I was going to sit, in front where everyone could admire me.

Oiseau smiled sweetly.

"Well, I'm going to ignore you completely and utterly. I'm the cuddly friend to have around here, not you ... you jumped-up piece of fluff. Your beak's far too long!! Not to mention the fact that you're skinny."

I'd been rude about Casey being jealous and now here was I, acting the same. Oh, Flippin' Flippers! I resolved that I really would talk to Casey about it when we got home.

Whatever. I'm still not going to speak to Oiseau.

I was so busy being cross that I missed the loveliness of the journey out, all the fun of staying in a caravan in the snow and the excitement of walking on skis across challenging mountain slopes.

It wasn't until I found myself helping to dig a large hole in a high snowy bank, that I realised I needed to change my thoughts to something more positive. I was being my own worst enemy. OK, use a mantra ... Cool Fish! Cool Fish! Cool Fish! Cool Fish!

I felt better immediately. Good technique!

Sleeping in the snow-hole was fun. In fact, just the sort of thing that penguins love. Our own special snow cave carved to the specifications we wanted and snug from the weather outside. And we could peer out and see down onto the sparkling lights in the valley below.

But I felt sorry for Oiseau that night. She wasn't an experienced adventurer like me.

"I feel like a lump of ice," she said.

"Well, that's the problem with being so skinny. Here, you can lean up against me if you like."

Well, there's not much point in being a superhero if you can't be gallant with it, is there?

There was something about meeting Oiseau that made me feel braver and more up for what I had to do.

Returning home, first I had to answer a hundred questions from Footie. Then I decided this was the moment. Casey and the gang were lolling about indifferently as usual.

"Er ... Casey ... eh, actually there's something I want to say."

"Ready for a beating?" interrupted one gang member.

"Well ... actually it's ..."

"OK! Let's hear it."

"Um ... I don't know how to say this ... Um ... I know I've been arrogant and loud-mouthed. I'm sorry. I'm sorry to all of you. I would like us to be friends."

I waited to be shouted down.

Instead, there was a stunned silence. Then ...

"That's OK, mate," said Casey.

"We're sorry, too," said two others.

"You're cool, really," said a third. "So tell us about this little bird."

It was as easy as that. Just the need to be brave. And honest. Who would have thought? To be accepted into the gang gave me such a sense of belonging. It was as though an enormous weight had been lifted from my shoulders. I knew something important had happened. I'd changed how I was and that had changed the whole situation.

Could it be that the whole wide world could be changed in this way?

That summer found us with another chance to try the Matterhorn. Cool Fish! I had wanted to avenge our previous failure for a long time now.

"We have a special job to do," My Human said. "I made a promise to my old friend, the one who just died. She'd climbed the Matterhorn when she was young and it was the most important event of her life. We have to carry her ashes to the summit to spread them onto the mountain, in order to honour her life."

Well, that seemed appropriate. And, nothing like carrying a bit of extra weight up a mountain ...

When the Boyfriend came to pick us up in the car, bulging with adventuring equipment as usual, I saw that Oiseau wasn't hanging from the front windscreen. Where is she? Was she OK?

"Oiseau's decided not to come this time."

Oh, no. Flippin' Flippers! I hadn't realised I'd wanted her to be there so much. I suppose I had been quite rude to her last time. I felt like a rock was in my stomach. What was that feeling all about?

I was so busy feeling sorry for myself that I didn't notice the commotion going on at the ferry terminal, when we were waiting to cross the channel to France.

"I'm sorry but I've left the ashes behind," said My Human. "We'll have to go back."

"That's another four hours' drive! You idiot! Means we'll miss the ferry and have to drive through the night."

There was a lot of glaring and gnashing of teeth. Humans!

By the time we'd retraced our steps and were in the Alps at last, things seemed more peaceful. I figured the air had cleared when they dressed up for dinner in the tent – she in a long dress and he in a bow tie. Boring!

Anyway, I thought I'd better help things along and have a word with the nature fairies. I knew how important the weather was for this climb. Hard, cold snow and bare rocks are relatively safe. Anything in between can be dodgy.

The weather turned perfect. We set off in the darkest hour of the night ... aiming for the highest.

"You'll be pleased to hear I've remembered to bring the ashes," My Human said.

The good conditions meant there were lots of other people on the mountain, which not only slowed us down, but increased the danger of rock-fall. We did make good progress through the day; however, by the time the light was fading we'd still only reached an angled bit known as the shoulder, with an hour to go to reach the summit.

"I know I'm very slow," My Human said, "even with superhero flipper assistance."

"If we continue, we'll have to sleep out on the mountain," said the Boyfriend.

There was only one safe thing to do.

My Human poured the ashes out of the urn onto their final resting place on the shoulder of the mountain. The wind came and scattered them like a passing cloud, the ghost of yesteryears.

The long hard journey down into the night was full of heavy disappointment. I felt empty.

My Pegbert was hurt and sullen. I couldn't believe it. Another failure! What was I going to tell my new friends in the gang? More to the point, what was I going to tell Oiseau? Superheroes are meant to be successful.

The following morning near the base hut we stopped to look at a new plaque nailed into the rock. It read: THIS MOUNTAIN HAS BEEN DEDICATED TO PEACE.

Hmm ...That makes me think of other people, not just myself. I know it's just my Pegbert that feels so let down. I can be humble. We were lucky enough to be on the mountain, and we were able to send off the friend's ashes, even if it wasn't at the top. We've returned safely. And there was always the next adventure.

By seeing the positives of the bigger picture I found it was possible to accept how things were and move on. This filled up the hollow feeling inside. And it made one thing very clear. For sure, I wasn't going to be beaten. I would give everything I had the next time ... and the next after that.

I spoke to Footie and the gang about it when I got home. "This character building stuff sure is hard work, you know. I s'pose you're going to tell me there's treasure in failure ..."

"The treasure is in how you pick yourself up and start again," said Footie. "Ye Gods, man, you should be learning that by now."

"Determination to keep going is a pretty useful treasure, mate," said Casey. "Better than this fickle fame stuff."

I guess ...

I wanted to talk to Oiseau about it, to tell her that I'd found the Determination treasure, and what a superhero I was in spite of the second failure on the Matterhorn. Indeed, that instead of getting me down it had motivated me to be more persistent than ever. But she didn't come on the next adventure, either.

In some ways I was glad, because this was serious business. By now I was part of Climb For Tibet, which My Human and the Boyfriend had set up. I'm officially My Human's PA (Penguin Assistant, for those who don't know). We raise funds to build schools in Tibet and collect peace messages from humans all over the world to send off from far high places, in the Tibetan tradition of flying prayer flags to send out peace and harmony. Our intention is to express the peaceful Tibetan way of helping the earth.

The first peace climb was to the earth's furthest point which is, interestingly, a mountain in Ecuador. Part of me wished that Oiseau would be there on the climb. In view of what happened, it was a good thing she wasn't.

It was a painful adventure. I put my whole self into it to help the world. And what happened? I ended up as sacrificial fodder. All I ever ask of My Human is that I can be with her. Yet she abandoned me on the mountain at a very crucial stage of the climb. She had all sorts of reasons, like her brain was exploding and she knew she was going to die. But so what? That's no excuse for abandoning your best penguin, is it?

Anyway, Dear Reader, you can find the story, if you want to, in My Human's book called *Cry From The Highest Mountain*. Suffice to say I forgave her the minute she rescued me. So long as she never leaves me again.

This deepened my determination to never, ever be beaten – not to let things get me down.

This was to prove more useful than I could ever have dreamed.

ONENESS

WITH LOVE THERE IS NO SEPARATION

Thankfully, after this setback, there was an exciting party to focus on. It was time to move on and prepare for the new millennium, the beginning of a new thousand-year span. You're not going to get many of those in your lifetime, are you?

All round the world celebration plans were being hatched.

"I hope we're going to do something meaningful that'll bring *oomph* to the planet," I said to the gang.

"Listen to you, mate," said Casey. "You're growing up. You're thinking of everybody else now."

"And you're using all those hard-won treasures," said Footie. "But Ye Gods, remember – the tougher the next adventure, the better the treasure is bound to be."

Hmm ...

I had celebrated New Years Eves before, of course, midnight parties decorated with sparkly tinsel on mountain tops. But this one had to be extraordinary.

It needed to be a special place at this very special time.

In a bid to collect the messages that were expressions from the highest place in people's hearts (ie, the most spiritual), and send them off from the highest place possible (in the reachable world), My Human and the Boyfriend decided, "We'll do a peace climb to the point on earth nearest the sun at the millennium."

Wooh! Sounded great. But a little complicated. The point nearest the sun varies on a day-to-day basis within the tropics. Over the millennium change it was to be the highest point on a special latitude south of the equator – for seventeen seconds at 1.35pm. Flippin' Flippers, seventeen seconds! This will certainly be a blink-and-you'll-miss-it sort of time and place. And a good idea not to be late, rather than to have to wait around for another thousand years.

Searching on maps revealed that the highest point on this latitude was a mountain over six thousand metres tall situated in northern Chile close to the Bolivian border, which nobody had ever heard of. Sounded like we'd be heading to South America again. Cool Fish!

"Things are more powerful with a team," said My Human, so she went about gathering individuals interested in joining us. She wanted the climb to be a symbolic gesture to help world peace. "We need to have both a Tibetan and a Chinese person with us. Having representatives from two nations that are at odds with each other will demonstrate international brotherhood."

Our young Tibetan friend, who she had a close connection with, was persuaded to come. His parents had escaped out of Tibet with the Dalai Lama after the invasion by China.

Also onboard was a young Chinese, a refugee from the Tiananmen Square massacre when Chinese soldiers opened fire on a peaceful protest by students. We were proud to have both of them with us.

There were to be eight humans in all, mostly novice climbers. The Boyfriend was tearing his hair out with the thought of how to train everybody up, but managed to arrange some mountaineering practice in Britain and the French Alps.

Personally I don't mind how much hair he tears out so long as he brings Oiseau on the climb. Please, dear Boyfriend, please bring Oiseau ...

Everyone worked hard collecting peace messages from anybody they met. These varied from prayers, to sayings, to pledges, to wishes – each a special message that individuals wanted to send to the earth.

"It's an honour to carry these heartfelt thoughts," said My Human who took the responsibility very seriously. None more so than the messages from a group of children, all of whom had terminal cancer. I watched her reading a few, deeply moved. "I will not fear tomorrow ... Please look after my Mummy ... I want peace on earth ..."

All the messages were inscribed onto biodegradable rice paper to be sent off from the summit of the mountain. This meant a lot of work but everyone was dedicated to the cause of helping the greater good.

My Pegbert was surprisingly quiet around this preparation time. Was my compassion treasure starting to pay off for good?

Not long before we left, Britain had a visit from the Chinese president. I went with some of the team to London to join demonstrators waving Tibetan flags and heatedly shouting slogans protesting against the behaviour of the Chinese Communist government.

The government had marched into the country of Tibet claiming it as their own, killing a sixth of the population, destroying the religion including all the monasteries, stealing its resources, ransacking the environment and the unique culture and still ... still half a century later, contrary to their propaganda, oppressing the people.

The Tibetans fiercely support their exiled Dalai Lama who works tirelessly for world peace and encourages his people to resolve the problem without violence – a supreme example of Soft Courage. We are honoured that he is the patron of our Climb For Tibet.

We managed not to get arrested on the protest in London and importantly, to get a copy of all the thousands of peace messages to a Chinese official who promised to pass them on to his president – a passing on of harmony and hope.

"We cannot go backwards in life, but we can find a way to move forward together," said My Human with a heavy sigh. "My heart bleeds for the Tibetans – it's bothered me all my life. I've got nothing against the Chinese people themselves, but surely it's time to stop the oppression."

I was more concerned about the inevitable film footage of us demonstrating outside the Chinese Embassy. Now that I'm on the list of suspect penguins under surveillance with a national security record, would I be allowed out of the country for our pending climb?

It wasn't the security record that caused the problem at the airport on the way to Chile. The problem was a very special lantern, one that was carrying the essence of the World Peace Flame.

The World Peace Flame, lit with sacred intention by peace-makers around the earth and morphed to one flame in Wales, is blessed to burn eternally as something greater than the sum total of its parts. Candles and lanterns lit from this flame, then extinguished, are sent out to be relit across the world, carrying powerful peace energy.

We'd been asked to be the first to carry it to South America for the peace of the planet. But it was confiscated. Alternative travel arrangements had to be made for it.

My Human slumped into her seat on the iron bird saying, "I'm glad they didn't find all the other stuff." Me too. I was the guardian of the little rucksack containing the sacred items which were to go into the *stupa* to be built out of rocks on the top of the millennium mountain. A stupa is a blessed Tibetan structure consecrated by housing sacred items. It acts as a bringer-in of special positive energy.

The smallest item was what bothered me. It was a stone. Not just any sort, but a pebble from the whale-rubbing beaches of Canada, where the orcas go to rub their tummies. It was coming with us to represent the animal kingdom. A certain penguin could've done that. However, I'm trying hard to be harmonious and compassionate towards the orcas. It is a measure of how far my character development has come.

Never mind. Actually there's only one thing I care about. Oiseau's here!

She was relaxing, delicate wings outstretched, on the back of the Boyfriend's green rucksack wearing a pretty necklace. We had a whole adventure with which to get to know each other. Not wanting to rush our friendship I casually said, "Hi, Oiseau. Good to see you." She smiled back sweetly. I felt all warm inside.

We came down over the wild Andes mountain range into the city of La Paz, in Bolivia. "The guidebook says this is a bustling Latin American stronghold that will take your breath away," My Human recounted. We were at four thousand metres in altitude, the highest capital city in the world.

"Just what we need to start the acclimatisation process," said the Boyfriend. He knew that the success of this venture rested entirely on the physiological adaption of the bodies of the team so that they could cope with the reduced oxygen above the six thousand-metre altitude we were aiming for.

This meant gradually spending more and more time high up during the four weeks that we had available. I should mention that penguins don't generally have such problems. We have enhanced oxygen storage capability. Indeed, Emperors can last for half an hour with one breath whilst diving in the sea.

Altitude adaption is a very individual, isolating thing. The humans one by one went through the process of adapting to the lack of oxygen – gasping for breath at the slightest exertion, feeling nauseous, weak, dizzy and headachy. Everyone made sure they slowed down and drank loads of water. None of it was easy, particularly as we were doing training climbs and making high camps to pick up vital survival skills.

I could see that we were a pretty inexperienced lot, but we all had the basic belief that what we were doing was helping save the earth, which was an important weapon in the fight to achieve our objective and would carry us through tough times.

The team thought we'd better follow the traditional belief here in La Paz, which was to head out in a boat on the sacred Titicaca, a vast high lake on the border with Peru, to make offerings to appease Great Oneness. This, we were told, would make sure that we had good conditions on our climb. No doubt the nature fairies were helping here.

The idea was to throw a dried llama foetus – or alternatively, one's most precious possessions – into the bright turquoise water. We went for the latter. Following sacrifices of final pieces of chocolate, valuable water, cocoa leaves and the special English bread called cowpat which My Human loved, the Boyfriend playfully tried to make an offering of My Human herself. She declined.

What could we do now to ensure good weather?

"You'd make a lovely offering," I said to Oiseau.

In return I received a stern glare. Oh dear. She was not amused and no amount of grovelling seemed to be able to make it up to her.

Flippin' Flippers. Females!

I hoped Christmas Day in a hotel in La Paz would make amends. It was about as memorable as it gets. At least it would have been if it hadn't ended up in an alcoholic haze. Either that or it was the altitude that got to me. One way or the other I only have vague recollections ... I remember well the excitement of the phone call to My Human's boys in England and giving out sweets to children in the streets.

I remember the Boyfriend in a red cap hunting for sherry, the presents and much merriment. I think I remember the young Chinese hugging the young Tibetan who then introduced me to a soft white lion. I dimly remember dancing on a table to the playing of panpipes. What I don't remember is how I ended up dressed in a shiny purple skirt, wrapped around with bright red tinsel and in a compromising position with Oiseau ...

Our Climb For Tibet family was a little worse for wear early the next morning as we gathered ourselves and our gear into two jeeps. Whatever had happened between me and Oiseau was bad enough for her not to want to talk to me ...

My Pegbert was intensely frustrated. This altitude thing certainly takes its toll.

Our journey to the millennium mountain took us south across a sweeping rocky desert. The roads were rutted gravel tracks and we became covered in dust, with everyone's tummy feeling like it was on a bucking bronco.

I was on My Human's rucksack next to the Young Tibetan, so between bumps I was able to speak with the new member of our team attached to his front. "I am a Tibetan snowlion," the soft toy explained. "In our folklore, snowlions symbolise fearlessness and victory over all obstacles. They are also said to leap from mountain peak to mountain peak."

He sounded just the sort of team member we needed.

"My name is Pema, like the young Tibetan's father," he said. "This name indicates strength. My job is to hold warmth, wakefulness and safety all the way up and down the mountain."

I liked him. He was open and friendly and – although undersized –obviously powerful. "How nice for you to be able to travel on the young Tibetan's front," I said, wishing for the first time in my life that I was smaller and could travel on My Human's front instead of always on her rucksack or harness.

"Yes. I guard his heart," he replied.

I had the feeling then that Pema the snowlion was a wise being. Something about the way he was gave me larger amounts of the courage treasure.

The next day we drove west across vast salt flats and onto tracks slippery from rain. The talk was of dangerously loose snow up on the volcanoes which now appeared – vast white-capped mountains pushing up out of a raw earth as we crossed over the border into Chile. The idea of a border between countries seemed totally irrelevant here, the most "nowhere" place imaginable.

Through heavy black cloud a compelling presence loomed. I glimpsed a floating white apparition. It was a massive dormant volcano – our millennium mountain.

We fought our way around rocks and patches of snow up its disused track until the vehicles could go no further. We were at an old sulphur mining camp, which seemed like the most desolate place on earth. Here amongst scattered bones was a broken-down cableway and a line of roofless stone buildings, perfect to shelter our tents from the wind. Base camp! At over five thousand metres!

As darkness fell the Young Chinese spotted a shooting star. If it hadn't been for the biting cold, relentless wind, smell of rotten eggs and the intense altitude sickness in the form of nausea and dizziness which the humans felt, all would have been perfect. I was happy anyway. Oiseau had decided to talk to me.

"I'm really scared by everything," she disclosed. She gave me what I found to be a very appealing look.

Superhero Yannick was there for her, all through the night as it happened, as My Human was awake, too, helping the Boyfriend who was having trouble breathing and was hyperventilating, which was making me scared, too.

We had three days to adapt to this higher altitude and test out part of the old track that zigzagged into an unknown horizon of snow towards the summit.

We established a gateway through which we would set off. On one side we flew sacred prayer flags, on the other the Tibetan flag and mani-stones which the young Tibetan made. Mani-stones are way-markers of flat rock engraved with the mantra *Om mani padme hum*, the magical Tibetan mantra of compassion.

Pema the snowlion quietly chanted the mantra. "Its resonance purifies for peace," he explained.

"Great millennium mountain, guardian of the stones," My Human spoke, "we come to bring gifts and a light for peace to your summit. We ask for strength and we ask for oxygen."

Thunder growled from a threatening sky. We had been acknowledged by the mountain.

In spite of the frequent storms playing in this wild auditorium belonging only to nature, that day the pure electricity in the air seemed to reach a peak. My Human suddenly cried, "My head is sizzling. I'm sure a thunder bolt has hit the top of it." I watched fascinated as light came off her hands whenever she touched something. Everyone else, too, seemed to be alive with electricity.

"Maybe it's the earth shifting and rebalancing," the young Tibetan said.

Oiseau was shaking with fright at being zapped on the Boyfriend's back.

"Don't be scared," comforted Pema the snowlion. "Fear only attracts that which is feared. Know that all is well."

The peace messages carried similar positive thoughts. To honour the sentiments written in the most powerful way, we were going to both speak them out at the gateway and physically let them off from the summit.

In relays, it took two continuous, cold, dedicated days to speak out over two thousand expressions, headed by the millennium message from the Dalai Lama. It read:

Let there be respect for the earth, peace for its people, love in our lives, delight in the good, forgiveness for past wrongs and from now on a new start.

Finally, the millennium change arrived. Bye-bye Old World. Hello New Start. This was it.

Early in the night snow fell heavily, blanketing our tent. I don't think anybody slept much. We waited. The wind stilled its normally incessant complaint at our invasion of its territory and there was an unusual quiet. The sky was clear. A million stars high above us would light our way.

The planned departure was in the darkest hour of the night. Our aim was the highest point of the millennium mountain. I worried if this would give us long enough in view of the exact time – 1.35pm – that we needed to be on the summit for the special seventeen seconds. That was the only time we would be at the point on earth nearest the sun over the twenty-four hours of the millennium change.

It was impossible to tell if we would have enough time to get there. But it was critical.

My Human and the Boyfriend prepared their rucksacks – including important passengers – in our tent.

"Go well, Oiseau." I said.

"You, too," she replied. "You know, being with you, Yannick, makes me feel braver."

I sighed happily. There certainly was something in this team-bonding thing that made everything better. I'd seen it every day in the humans, how they supported each other and took strength from each other.

Outside as the team gathered, the young Tibetan squeezed My Human's hand. Silent support. They knew what it was like in the dreaded zone above six thousand metres – the fight for oxygen, the sacrifices required, the focus of the mind to keep going. Pema the snowlion looked completely calm. I recognised his state of inner peace and wished I could be like that. I, myself, was jittery.

By the time everyone was ready, we were late setting off. We were a little line of eight head-torches snaking its way upwards, carrying the light into the darkness, soon to be joined by a watery half moon. There was no problem seeing the track in the snow. "We must stay together no matter what," said the Boyfriend, the most experienced one, with his eye firmly on the safety of the group. I was to wish later that we *had* stuck together.

We struck a steady, ever-onwards pace for a couple of hours until the dawn softly crept into the sky. The first sun of the new millennium was with us. A grey-pink sky turned to magenta and it was possible to make out the angle of the slope and the snow all around us, down to the campsite and beyond to the sculptured folds of the rusty brown earth falling away in a stunning display of the finest view imaginable. Yet all eyes were upwards ... waiting ... waiting 'til we could see what appeared to be the white dome of the summit high above us. Cool Fish!

A couple of hours further up we came across a ramshackle hut caked in dust where we took a rest. The altimeter read five and a half thousand metres. The humans tried to force in food and drink. This was where the Boyfriend discovered that My Human had mistakenly filled his bottle with something other than water. He took a swig and rapidly spat it out "Ugh!! That's paraffin!!" I thought it was hilarious!

He set off, but My Human waited for one of the team who was worried about frostbite in his cold toes. This meant that by the time we left the hut the others were ahead. We plodded steadily, following the footprints which moved away from the track, presumably to find a quicker route but this made it harder for us. By the time we caught up, the Boyfriend was roped up to the young Tibetan and the young Chinese.

My Human set up the other rope with the rest of the team, tying everyone on at intervals along it. But it seemed to take forever to unravel the rope and tie the knots. I watched tensely as Oiseau disappeared ahead with the faster team. We followed on behind more tentatively. We moved together where we could but it took more time still roped up and belaying where things looked dodgy. The going was steep and tough and demanded concentration. Onwards ever upwards.

The sun was now high in the sky and the humans were hot, so they had to stop and take off layers. I could see that My Human's face was burning. We were following the footprints of the others as the safest thing to do, but up ahead there was no sign of them at all.

Of course they'll wait for us. The Boyfriend had been so insistent that we all stay together, but the movement, the struggle and the hours went on and there was still no sight of them. I just wanted to arrive at the top with Oiseau.

Hmm. My Pegbert kicked in. I don't want her to get there before me. That's far more to the point. Doesn't do my image any good if the weak female beats the strong male.

I'm getting really agitated.

"It's important to be in the right frame of mind for the summit ceremonies," said My Human. "The peace messages have to be sent off with unconditional love. I'm trying hard to let go of my ego and not mind that the others haven't waited for us."

Pegbert went quiet.

We were all very tired now. The snow positively reeked of rotten egg smell from the volcano gases, and where there were yellow sulphur rocks the scent was worse. It was making My Human cough badly. But she was more concerned about the time. It was after midday. An hour or so to go and still a lot of ground to cover. She shouted encouragingly, "We're going to make it. Keep focused. Make every step count. Hang in there."

Then we spotted the others up ahead, half way up the final ridge.

Ah, at last! They must be waiting for us. But time was marching on ... Everyone's so tired and surely having to dig deeper within themselves than they thought possible.

I called to the nature fairies for assistance. Next minute it was as though a soft wind gathered from behind and blew us along. How did they manage to do that?

"We have angelic help, you know, lifting us up," called My Human. "All will be perfect timing, whatever. Use every reason of the mind to keep the body going. We can't not get there if the others do. Do it for the schools we're raising money for in Tibet. Do it for the earth and world peace. Do it for all the people who are sending love and support to us."

I knew she was thinking of her boys back at home. And I could tell, even though her body was prepared for the altitude, that her mind was less acclimatised: her thoughts were starting to drift.

And the sun beat down. And the point nearest the sun was getting closer.

"C'mon. You can do it!" I heard. Ah, it was Pema the snowlion. We must have caught the others up. But I looked around and there was no sign of them. "C'mon. You can do it!" I heard again. Funny ...

Then My Human turned saying, "Wow! I've just heard the young Tibetan saying, 'C'mon. You can do it' as though he was standing beside me. I must be hallucinating."

What strange magic was this?

I could see that the young Tibetan's voice had given My Human the boost she needed. "Half an hour to go!" she shouted and moved into a steady rhythm – breathing deeply, wheezing, panting.

Repeat. Following the footprints upwards towards the summit dome.

"Twenty minutes!" Closer and closer. The others must be there. Onwards ...

"Five minutes!"

It was possible, I found, to sense how everyone on the rope was feeling – completely done in. Giving their all. Suffering inwardly. Then the rope was pulled taut and stopped. One of the team was faltering badly.

"Please. Let's keep going. We'll miss the time," My Human pleaded.

"You untie and keep going," came the reply.

"No, I'm not untying anything. We're all getting there together."

With much yanking of rope, everyone staggered over the brow of the summit, where the others were gathered. Someone offered to take My Human's pack, but she wanted to carry the sacred items herself on this last leg of the climb and kept going.

Go! Go! Flat out to the summit point, the centre of a wide open gently-sloping dome with patches of rock, six thousand metres into the sky. We got there. The time: 1.45pm.

Ten minutes late.

Flippin' Flippers!

Ten minutes late!

Did it matter?

Oh yes, with every bit of my being it mattered. All those months of preparation – all that supreme effort – how could we come all this way and be ten minutes late? And Oiseau had got there ahead of me. And on time.

Pegbert was livid. I'm disappointed, frustrated, annoyed and most of all inexplicably angry at Oiseau. Flippin' Flippers!

How am I ever going to find the right state of mind to do the crucial summit jobs?

Everyone was trying to hug everyone else, unable to believe how hard it had been and that we'd actually made it. My Human sat down and burst into tears. That's just what she does at the top of mountains, I suppose.

I tried to take in the view of this most stunning of places, part of a raw earth stretching in every direction with volcano-tops and desert that went on seemingly forever. We were here. We'd made it. But there was emotional chaos going on inside me.

I spotted Pema the snowlion watching me. "It's OK, you know," he said kindly. "The young Tibetan pushed hard in spite of extreme back pain and was at the top first. He called *Om mani padme hum* seventeen times during the correct seventeen seconds, on behalf of the entire team. He was in exactly the right state of mind, the Tibetan way of unconditional love for all beings. That was precisely what was needed."

I felt humbled and ashamed. I realised that if the others had waited for us then none of the team would've made it in time. And that would have been unthinkable.

"The *team* got here," said Pema. "Because we are all one."

I looked around and things became clearer. Suddenly it was not so important to be me, to be Yannick Penguin. There was a sense of the coming together of individuals to become one – to become the team that Pema was talking about. I could feel what everyone else was going through.

Oiseau was looking pale and limp on her rucksack. "Well done," I said to her a bit sheepishly.

The Boyfriend was gasping "I need water ... It was so hard kicking those steps in the snow. But all I wanted to do was get us to the top."

"Yes," said the young Chinese. "That last bit was impossibly hard. I made it, thanks to the team and particularly the young Tibetan encouraging me ... And you know what? I think I've changed. I've found an awakening to a spiritual dimension which I thought had been lost. I hope my brothers and sisters in China can find the same."

With that, My Human wrapped him and the Young Tibetan in the Tibetan flag. She then took a photo of China and Tibet, hand-in-hand in brotherhood.

"Real peace," said the young Chinese.

He and the young Tibetan hugged My Human and started chanting. The others joined in around them. It seemed to bring a powerful calm. Then My Human held her hands up to the sun saying, "Here at this point of harmony between earth and sun at the millennium, we reach for the light and release two thousand peace messages in the spirit of Tibet, for the peace of the earth and the harmony of nations."

Her hands were shaking as though energy was coming from the golden orb in the sky through them and down into the depth of the mountain. I could see countless nature fairies skipping blissfully, and a rainbow halo around the sun.

It was the right moment for everyone to bring out their packets of peace messages so lovingly conceived and carefully inscribed onto biodegradable rice paper and to throw them upwards, releasing them dancing onto the now gentle winds. In the days to come they would be carried far and wide, taking peace and harmony across the planet in the way of the Tibetan windhorse.

Then it was time for the sacred offerings. I had doubts that the precious World Peace Flame lantern would work here where there is only half of the amount of oxygen in the air compared to at sea level. But amazingly, the Boyfriend lit it to shine for a brief moment before lowering it into its final resting place deep in the rocks beneath the snow.

The lantern was joined by all the other items, including a tiny disc containing the messages, and the whale stone. Ah, the whale stone ... the orcas. I have to hold compassion. I stared at the stone as it went in, reciting *Om mani padme hum.*

Phew! Powerful thing this compassion. Made it without balking. Wow!

A lovely stupa of rocks was built over the offering place. Peace for all time from the point nearest the sun at the millennium.

It was becoming very cold. The team turned to go.

Oiseau gave me a smile that burnt itself into my heart, saying "I'll never forget this experience we shared ..."

Pema the snowlion winked at me and said, "Better not be late next time ..."

It had been a hard lesson. But yes, I felt happy for us all and had seen that there was something more important than my separate self. It was about everyone working together for the common good as one family. The treasure shining through was Oneness.

How was I ever going to live up to that?

"This treasure's a bit awe-inspiring," I said to my friends back at the cottage. "It's like finding out that I'm something much bigger than myself, but not knowing how to be it."

"Why bother, mate?" asked Casey, "There's a lovely comfy sofa here. And you can sit and look cuddly with the rest of us."

"Well, actually, now I feel more determined than ever to go and find the answer and build a better me," I said.

"You just like the challenge of the adventuring."

"Sure, but there's also a lot of work to do to help the world."

"Ye Gods," said Footie. "Surely the earth is saved by now."

"Not yet. The world needs peace, and I think we can each help it with our state of mind. How we are ourselves affects the behaviour of others. Our moods seem to be catching."

"Yo, Yannick! Slow down a bit... Ah ... I s'pose we can all work to find inner peace, even superhero penguins!"

"You're right," I said. "But I feel there's something restricting me. It's as though I'm not free to be what I want to be. I need to keep searching. I think when I find that freedom, I'll find the answer."

INSIGHT

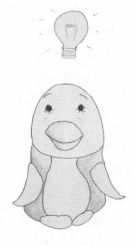

FREEDOM COMES FROM WITHIN

Freedom ... Hmm. But what about the answer to freedom in Tibet? Tibetans don't have freedom in their own occupied country. There was much distressing news, like the stories of innocent monks and nuns beings gaoled and tortured. And the forced sterilisation of female humans ...

So it felt good that we were able to do something positive to help. We quietly arranged for the building of two entire schools in Tibet with the sponsorship funds raised from the Millennium Climb.

"Why don't we go and see them?" said My Human. "I've always had the deepest yearning to go to Tibet."

Me, too. Bet there's never been a penguin in Tibet before. I'll probably get mistaken for a baby yeti, and they'll start writing legends about me. Cool Fish!

"Hopefully we'll get in," said the Boyfriend. "But the borders are often closed to foreigners. And anyway, even with visas we might be stopped because of our connections with the Dalai Lama."

Perhaps a penguin decoy would help ... on the other hand, perhaps not one on the list of suspect penguins with a national security record. I might just lie low and help by visualising us there.

But the humans started months of preparation, arranging a journey. Three thousand new peace messages were collected from individuals wanting to create a more positive, sustainable and peaceful world.

All the messages were to be spoken out three times, once from each of three designated mountains – Kailas, the holiest of high mountains; Shishapangma, the highest completely in Tibet; and Everest, the highest above sea level. We would be deep in the Himalayas, the highest mountain range on earth.

Surely this was every penguin's dream – well, every superhero penguin anyway. But would we be allowed in?

We left at the beginning of summer. It should have been perfect, but there was a hole in my excitement.

Oiseau didn't come. I suppose she really didn't have the stamina for these sorts of adventures. She'd had the stuffing knocked out of her on the last one. But it was as though part of me was missing ... I resolved to make her proud of me by working further on my character development.

My Human, the Boyfriend and I flew to Kathmandu in Nepal, a country steeped in poverty with warm and lovely people, and were driven north towards the border with Tibet. All being well we were heading into a country filled with magical legends of mystery and wonder. We had to be prepared for anything.

I considered that with all the huge challenges Tibet has been through and continues to go through, surely it must be filled to the brim with treasure.

A long narrow bridge stretched from Nepal to Tibet, poised high over a deep gorge with a churning river below. It was eerily empty. We set off to walk across, porters carrying our bags. In the middle of the bridge was a white line. We stepped gingerly over it into Tibet.

After further steps My Human took a photo and dropped an offering over the side of the bridge onto Tibetan soil on behalf of the young Tibetan who had come with us on the Millennium Climb. His mother had not wanted him to join us on this trip. Although it had been his dearest wish, the chances of being arrested and never seen again had been too risky.

Suddenly, Chinese soldiers appeared, shouting at us angrily, "No photo! No photo!" We were escorted to the far side of the bridge, where we showed our papers.

They let us pass. We were in!

Walking past a few Chinese stalls selling plastic goods, we were greeted in the traditional Tibetan manner with *"Tashi Delek"* and white scarves were placed round our necks by an engaging local guide.

The guide was to be with us for the next two months, along with the rest of his Tibetan team: a young cook and two drivers for a land-cruiser and a truck bringing tents, food, petrol and all that we would need. Tibet doesn't really have things like shops, at least not as a well brought-up penguin knows them.

The team spoke good English and we warmed to them immediately.

"Where are you from?" My Human asked the guide.

"Lhasa, capital of Tibet," he said.

"Are there many Chinese in Lhasa?" asked the Boyfriend.

The guide looked furtively over his shoulder, obviously afraid of Chinese ears "There are some things I can't tell you," he said. "We have to be careful. A good friend of mine, who was a guide too, lost his job because one of his clients had a picture of the Dalai Lama. Jobs are very hard to come by for us Tibetans. We must ask you to be cautious, but try to hold compassion, too."

We were taken up the steep side of the gorge through thick green and abundant jungle to a little town. There was a stark contrast between the collections of small houses, many of them hovels, and a few large concrete official buildings, like the Chinese hotel we had to spend the night in, whilst we and our papers were scrutinised.

I'm still lying low. I know nothing.

Thankfully, the next day we were allowed to set off in the vehicles. We tackled an unstable track winding its way upwards clinging to the side of the gorge so close to the edge that peering over was as the guide said, "difficult to tell if you're in this world or the next".

The edges of things became blurrier still as altitude sickness kicked in for My Human and the Boyfriend. There was no acclimatisation left from the millennium trip. By the time we'd climbed to four and a half thousand metres over a high pass strewn with colourful faded prayer flags and turned west onto the gigantic Tibetan plateau that stretched in all directions, they were both feeling horrible.

They barely bothered to eat and collapsed gratefully into our tent each night. For the next few days the open grassland we crossed became dryer and dustier until it was rocky desert, with little more than herds of goats, sheep and yaks for company. It was easy to see how useful the indigenous yak was, foraging in this high barren land.

But we may as well have been travelling across the moon for all the interest My Human and the Boyfriend took, lying back clutching their tummies except when being sick out the window. I felt sorry for them. At least I enjoyed the wild freedom of the landscape.

I don't think they appreciated either the cultural significance of stopping for a nice cup of tea. This took place in a restaurant, which was a grey tent with an iron stove that was fuelled by yak and sheep dung.

Here, a kettle was boiled that contained a hunk of tea leaves and salt, which was then mixed with yak butter in a churn and poured through a white scarf – presumably catching odd bits of yak dung – into a flask.

The tea was served in bowls as they sat on benches beside a beautiful painted chest. If they didn't drink up, the bowls were physically picked up and put to their lips. When they'd taken a sip the bowls were refilled again immediately. Tibetan yak butter tea is the social thing to drink.

You'd have thought they'd realise how rude it was to blame tummy sickness and rush away from the tent.

Sometimes the road followed the banks of a great river. We could see small settlements on the other side. Near one we had to stop at a Chinese check point. The guide was in trouble because our truck was ahead of us and the rules were that it had to be behind the land-cruiser we were in. We watched him give our papers to two military policemen, who stared at us sternly.

Nearby was a group of poor-looking Tibetans with a dog. The dog wandered over and sniffed around. A policemen took out his electric baton and started electrocuting the dog, who yelped in pain. The other policeman laughed and thought it a great joke.

The Boyfriend shouted at the policeman to stop. The guide grabbed our papers, jumped into our vehicle and called to the driver to go quickly before we were all detained. My Human – moved to tears by the cruelty – declared, "Now I see how they can torture the monks and nuns."

Flippin' Flippers! We were going to have to behave ourselves here. And somehow rise to the challenge of holding compassion for the Chinese officials.

Was that going to be possible?

After nearly a week of driving I knew the humans were feeling human again, as they were excited at drawing close to Mount Kailas. But before that, the plan was to undertake a walk around Tibet's most sacred lake, called Manasarovar.

We came around the brow of a mountain past a little monastery rebuilt precariously into a steep rocky hill overlooking a magnificent sight – a great expanse of water of the brightest turquoise blue, surrounded by snow-capped mountains.

Cool Fish!

I was struck by the magical feel of Manasarovar, as though there was a powerful force that emanated from it that I didn't understand. Certainly its water has far-reaching effects for millions of beings, as near here is the source of Asia's four greatest rivers.

The wind rippled across the surface of the lake in greeting. As we pitched our tents on the sandy shore I felt an irresistible urge to speak with the nature fairies, who were gathering in gangs around us. I didn't seem to be consciously calling them up any more. They were just there.

However, these nature fairies appeared to be really agitated about something. They wanted reassurance from me. Yes, we come with peace in our hearts. Yes, we honour this sacred land. For some reason this was important to them. Perhaps it's just that they were bewildered to find a penguin so far off course from his natural habitat.

The humans sat on fold-up chairs and dined on the usual rice, onions and cabbage which the Boyfriend found boring but My Human loved, especially as she supplemented it with some olive oil and yeast extract which they'd brought with them. The team were also happy to have gleaned some yak meat.

The guide told us, "The lake is so important to millions of Hindus that their tradition is to immerse themselves in it for cleansing and healing. Even some of Gandhi's ashes are spread here. But for those of us who are Buddhists, merit is gained by walking around it. It'll take three days. It's only fifty-five miles."

The guide was really excited to be here. After all, in this land-locked land he'd never had the experience of seeing an ocean, so this was the biggest expanse of water he'd ever visited. Coming from the British Isles, this was hard for me to imagine.

"I'm glad our team's not Hindu," said the Boyfriend. "Looks a bit chilly for swimming. There's lumps of ice floating about."

Well, I thought it looked rather inviting ...

At sunrise we set off in a clockwise direction with the nature fairies giving us their blessing. The sky was the clearest blue imaginable. All around us was the sound of water birds. A little fox was watching a guinea-pig shaped mouse. Marmots bounded. Further on we spotted chiru antelope up high, earlier we'd seen a wolf and a rare ibex. Later on, a herd of wild horses came down in front of us to drink.

It was as though we'd been accepted into this beautiful land which had given little outward signs of greenery and life. From the back of My Human's rucksack I happily watched nature fairies darting about on the waves that lapped gently on the shore as though saying, yes – separate, but part of the whole.

It was so lovely and harmonious I felt I was the luckiest penguin on the planet.

Towards evening the humans had to take their boots off and wade through a river brimming with large fish. "Look, snow-trout," said the guide ecstatically. He bashed one with a stone and brought it to us for dinner.

But later, when we came to the camp that the drivers had established, he was distraught. "I've never taken life before," he bemoaned. "I thought it would feed the team, but I feel so guilty. Usually it's only snow-trout bones we take from this lake as they're considered sacred and good to grind up for medicine that cures all ills. Now I've spoilt my inner peace."

"Your intention was to help others," replied the cook. "Your karma will be OK."

"At the next monastery I shall light a lamp for the fish's soul to have a good rebirth."

The Boyfriend with his generous nature gave the guide the olive oil and yeast extract as a means to cheer him up. The loss of precious supplies caused My Human to look exceedingly cross.

After the next stunningly beautiful day with a further exhausting eleven hours walking, we welcomed a visitor to our camp. It was a Chinese soldier, from a nearby army site. We were no longer surprised when they appeared as if from nowhere.

He brought a gift for our Tibetan team – snow-trout bones. To him they meant nothing, but he knew they were important to the Tibetans. As I watched him playing cards for a while with our team I realised he had restored my faith in the nature of humans. The compassion of the individual Chinese person was simply ... well, human. It was the Chinese system that was causing all the trouble.

The third day would have been another blissful time in one of the earth's most pristine wildernesses held in sacredness by the hearts of an entire people. Except for one thing. As we were approaching the last few miles we heard a sound.

The sound gradually became louder and it was apparent that it was a machine, a water pump. We came around a cliff to see a large pipe in a deep channel leading from the lake down into a pit and across to two large tents covering up some sort of heavy equipment with wires leading into it.

I couldn't believe that this natural paradise had been allowed to be defiled in this way. No wonder the nature fairies had been acting so strangely. In spite of the exhaustion of the long walk, we rushed back to the campsite on the sandy beach.

"What is it? What is going on?"

"It's the Chinese taking gold back to Beijing," explained the guide sadly. "The local people are desperate, but what can they do?"

"They've been pumping the water for three years now," said the cook. "It's lowering the lake and affecting the runoff into the lake nearby, which also has great significance for the Tibetan people."

My disbelief turned to anger at this greed.

Pegbert had a field day. What utter disrespect both to the earth and to the millions of humans that considered this place so sacred. Flippin' Flippers! What I could achieve with a few grenades ...

Whoops! That's not a very compassionate thought, is it? I need to try and learn some of the compassion of the Tibetans.

This sad, beautiful land was filling me to the brim

with tests. Different ones every day. So long as I don't overflow ...

Across the lake, Mount Kailas called to us. The mountain is said to accelerate paths of learning. Just what I need.

From a distance it looked like a perfect pyramid of shining snow rising above the grey of the surrounding mountains. Asians considered this the ultimate place of pilgrimage, the meeting point of heaven and earth. This was not just any old mountain.

I was determined to use all my hard-won treasures to keep Pegbert quiet and tackle it in the humble and conscious state of mind required ... trying to be aware of what I was doing ... trying to find some inner peace ... trying to be courageous ...

As we drove closer I could see that it was quite isolated. Its high point at nearly seven thousand metres was immaterial to us, though the subject of many magical legends, as it has always been forbidden for anyone to stand on its sacred summit.

Instead, the standard pilgrimage involves doing the *kora*, which means walking around it in a clockwise direction. It is said that to go around the mountain one hundred and eight times is to reach enlightenment.

We only had time for one kora, which was going to take us three days. But even once was important. By dint of its toughness, once is about purification, and said to erase the misdeeds of a lifetime.

Ah, how useful! Pegbert jumped in. I wonder what extra misdeeds I can get up to before we start.

Flippin' Flippers! Already my resolutions have been blown.

We gathered in a little encampment with other pilgrims before setting off, hiring yaks to carry our gear. The yak is not only Tibet's transport system, but also its dairy, butchers, fabric shop and a friend to be decorated with brightly coloured tassels.

I liked the yak. Those that looked after them, the yakpas, piled them high with all our gear, but I had the distinct feeling that if the yaks didn't want to move in a certain direction then nothing would make them. Well, if we never saw any of our gear again then we'd be the same as most Tibetans, not attached to much and travelling much the lighter for it.

Leaving the vehicles and drivers at the encampment we started out on foot and asked for blessings from the mountain, which threw us a beautiful auspicious rainbow. Taking a well-worn track west and then north past piles of mani-stones we followed the yaks, yakpas and a straggling gang of humans past a tall flagpole into a spectacular, rocky steep-sided valley. The only sign of habitation was a grey-brown monastery perched high on a ledge. It was quickly swallowed by the immensity of the natural systems in charge of this deep valley with rock-falls on either side and the glowing mountain dominating the skyline ahead.

I knew I was part of something so imposing, so much greater than myself it was almost as though I became it. I felt like I was in a film, with drum rolling, echoing chant of haunting voices, stunning scenery and then ... the penguin superhero riding on his yak. Yo, Yannick! You've finally saved the earth ... Well, at least I was enjoying the film. Being at altitude does funny things to your head.

We journeyed some way down the dramatic valley and passed a young Tibetan woman with a typical round dirty face and gleaming teeth. She waved My Human over to join her for a nice cup of

Tibetan tea. She smiled at me and I felt a lovely sense of friendship. My Human chatted happily with her, without similar language, but with obvious respect.

For whilst we was walking round the thirty-five miles, the Tibetan woman was prostrating round. This involved taking a step, putting hands on head, on neck and heart and then lying flat on the ground with arms outstretched. Then standing up, taking the next step and doing the whole process all over again. Its purpose is to lay down suffering and to purify all beings. That's dedication. The guide said that on top of that the woman had walked seven hundred miles for two months to get here from Lhasa.

That night it snowed heavily. I felt sorry for the yaks – all they seemed to have to eat was a mossy sort of cushion plant. But the cook made some wonderful breakfast pancakes for our team. They would need it. It was bitterly cold and there was a lot of uphill travel ahead.

Our aim was to reach the North Face of Kailas, a place of power, where it's said that one can plant one's deepest wish for the world and all the nature fairies will see to its accomplishment. Here was the perfect place for speaking out our peace messages. This was a mountain that amplifies prayers.

We clambered steadily uphill, heads held low through violent snow-showers, until the track turned east. The North Face came partly into view, a powerful presence guarded by an intimidating cloud. Nearby was a small building made from the surrounding rocks, the Female Yak Horn monastery. Here we were welcomed by the abbot in maroon robes and two smiley monks and invited in through a large second-storey window.

There was very little of anything physical inside the monastery, but the atmosphere was extraordinary. The tiny shrine room where all the meditations take place held so much intense compassion, it was like being safe in the womb of an egg, and made me wish I could stay there forever.

Our peace messages were spoken out under the blessings of the abbot and the biggest gang of nature fairies I've ever seen, in the aura of the mighty Kailas. My Human lit a World Peace Flame candle. I was filled up with deep stillness and contentment. *Om mani padme hum.*

It was an incredibly slow climb onwards up the steep snowy trail, at times scrambling across rocks. Our team were well acclimatised now but other humans plodded like penguins with wooden legs.

Flippin' Flippers, they were slow! At least this speed was useful to help hold the inner peace.

Along the way we saw strange piles of discarded clothes and were told that this represented the impermanence principle of letting go of the old, or of non-clinging. My Human decided she would hang onto all her stuff saying, "I definitely need it and I'm not going to litter this special place".

Reaching the highest point of the kora, at five and a half thousand metres, we found Tibetans throwing peace messages into the air and multiple strings of prayer flags flying. It was the going underneath the prayer flags at this point that signified the erasing of the misdeeds of a lifetime.

Cool Fish! Here we go. Ah! Actually I don't feel any different. Yet ...

Just on the other side, the Boyfriend started building the Climb For Tibet rock stupa in view of Kailas' glacier that was pouring down blessings. I was surprised that he was becoming agitated. It was only snowing lightly but the cold wind was numbing his hands and he was becoming upset by the many Tibetans trying to help but not placing the rocks the way he wanted.

Also, he was worrying about losing his rucksack and the objects for the stupa in this land where physical stuff seemed to be forever for sharing. Was there some sort of cleansing going on?

Eventually a fine, metre–high stupa reflecting the shape of the stupa of Kailas itself was finished and filled with precious objects, including a little disc of all the messages. It was consecrated with the help of the nature fairies to withstand the fierce mountain winds and do its work for peace for all time.

After the consecration, everything went downhill. It was a steep descent and we made good time. The Boyfriend went on speedily ahead whilst My Human walked more carefully. But it seemed for no reason she was agitated. She must have caught it off him. Inevitably then I caught it off her. I couldn't put a flipper feather on what it was, it was just that I felt out of sorts and part of the heavy grey cloud that was descending.

States of mind seemed to be very catching here.

After a while she stopped for a breather, took her rucksack off and sat down on a rock taking in the glimpses of the new view of the valley below us with some green vegetation. It seemed less grand on this side of the mountain. I felt grateful to have time without loads of other people around.

It didn't last for long. Two men came and sat close, on either side. One had a cream hat pulled tight down over his face. They started hassling My Human for money. They were trying to open her rucksack, pulling at her pockets and indicating that she should give them something. She started off smiling and being her usual friendly self, but then it became apparent they were being too pushy. I started feeling uneasy.

It was when she suddenly grabbed me with the rucksack and jumped up to face them that I became seriously afraid.

The men jumped up, too. One of them scowled at her menacingly. The one with the hat reached behind him to a long sheath and pulled out a knife.

Flippin' Flippers!

Flippin' Flippers!

How can something like this happen on a

sacred mountain? Was it because we were grumpy that we had attracted demons?

The man took a step towards us, brandishing his knife. I tried hard not to give in to the fear. What could I do? "Be cautious, but try to hold compassion," the guide had said, seemingly an eternity ago.

OK. I can do that. Cool Fish compassion! Cool Fish compassion! Cool Fish compassion ...

The next minute, thankfully, a young couple appeared over the horizon behind us. The two bandits spotted them and escaped down the mountain. We walked with the couple until we met up with the Boyfriend.

All through a restless night I felt out of sorts. I was cross with myself for losing my inner peace in such an important place. And that made me feel worse. It seemed that My Human was out of sorts, too. She was grumbling, "I've got no space. I'm cold and damp and I just want to be home."

In the morning the sun shone. It was warmer. The light reflected brightly off the river by our camp where a mist rose mysteriously out of the valley and a family of marmots stopped to talk to us. This day felt quite different to the previous day.

After a couple of hours walking we came across large piles of mani-stones, including mantras carved on yak-horns, directing us to the Miracle Cave monastery snuggled into Kailas' embrace. This one was built from the warm grey rocks but had wooden parts painted in faded colours: red for wisdom, white for compassion, black for protection.

My Human hesitated as to whether to go in. Just then a little girl called and came tripping down to meet us. She was around five years old, her hair tied into sticky-up bunches and with the smile of an angel. She grabbed My Human's hand, then one of my flippers and dragged us up to the monastery as though it was an everyday occurrence to have visiting penguins.

"Karma," she kept saying. I thought she was telling us her name. But as karma means what you give out you get back, I figured it was more likely to be the mountain asking us to look at our own karma.

She led us through a little courtyard, where other pilgrims were twirling prayer wheels, and into the building. There was a cave which was part of the shrine room where lamps flickered on an altar. This was a meditation refuge of Milarepa, the famous eleventh century poet and master.

After an early life filled with misdeeds, Milarepa took on the Buddhist teachings of discipline and the abandoning of material wealth and reached enlightenment. He was said to practise the magical arts of inner heat, only wearing a cotton sheet in the snow, and trance running without touching the ground.

The cave had the same intense compassion as had the last monastery. A chortling monk invited us to sit down on the mud floor and enter the stillness. I just had time to be aware of My Human shaking as though she was taking on unusual energy before I found myself flying in my mind higher and higher until I could feel that I wasn't a separate me anymore but had become all of this land of Tibet which was all of this beautiful earth. There were nature fairies with me riding the wind currents of the vision.

As I returned to the cave I felt the clear message: "Let go the demons of the mind. Freedom comes from within."

Outside, My Human tore some pages of paper from her diary as a gift for the little girl, and we wandered on, slowly following the river valley. A young pilgrim chatted to us as he walked by and My Human told him about the insight that she had just been given. "It was amazing. I went into a beautiful state of oneness, and was told that I'm isolating myself when I hang onto physical stuff."

The young man nodded wisely and moved on, obviously deep into his own thoughts.

We arrived back at the encampment having completed the kora and offered thanks to Kailas. We'd all been affected by our journeys. The Boyfriend spent time picking up everyone else's rubbish as though it was a way of giving back. My Human laughed when nearly arrested by soldiers whose photos she'd taken, as if ending up in a Chinese gaol didn't matter. I was busy trying to work out how this "freedom coming from within" thing worked.

But I felt excited to have found the treasure of Insight.

We met up again with our vehicles and headed east back along the great river. There was much beauty to enjoy. But I looked at the snowy Himalayan peaks knowing that we were free to go across them, and remembering that to Tibetans the mountains were forbidden barriers. They could only journey across secretly at night with no mountaineering clothes, in the winter, risking frostbite and possible death to order to reach freedom. Were they able to feel the freedom within?

HAPPINESS

The way to change a situation is to change your reaction to it

With an air of keen excitement we approached the lower slopes of our next giant Himalayan mountain. The vehicles could go no further, and so we needed a local carrier. The team tracked down two hairy yaks with their yakpas, who joined our camp to sit and relax watching the evening sun by a small dry riverbed.

One of the yakpas looked intently at the grassland around, while the guide translated what he told us. "You know last summer I was with six of my friends in just this spot grazing our yaks, and we saw a yeti over there."

I was only half listening, but at this I was all ears. (I do have cleverly streamlined ears!) Now we're talking. A yeti, a real live abominable snowman. Was this guy for real? I looked at him more closely.

He wore an old leather jacket. His long hair was tied up in typical fashion in a twirl of red wool with a white bone. He had a high forehead and intelligent eyes that were genuine and compassionate. Yes, I felt sure he was for real.

"He had the face of a man and long black hair all over his body, like a monkey. He was bending down, but after he spotted us he felt threatened and suddenly stood up as tall as a yak with horns. I was frightened."

"Could it be confused with another animal?" asked the guide.

Like an abominable giant penguin perhaps ...

"No. It was a yeti. That's the only time I'd seen one in this area, but there was his dung all over the valley which is like no other animal's dung."

"But if it was true, the government would send people to investigate," said the cook.

The yakpa shrugged. "I know the footprints. Same as a man's, but wider at the toe part. There's no heel. And five long fingers on the handprints that they use to pick up big stones while they search for small mammals underneath."

My Human's tea had gone cold. A silvery glow was beginning to cast long shadows across this wild terrain, a backdrop of intense beauty.

"We want to believe in these things," she mused. "It's part of the Shangri-La, the mythical land of paradise where all things are how we would like them to be. It's the impossible perfection ..."

I felt peaceful and very much part of the perfection.

But the sun was setting on a lost land that we all yearned for.

A new day always comes.

There was an unusual cloud in the eastern morning sky. The low light turned it salmon-pink and sparkling as if it had facets of crystal glass. I stared at it. Most definitely ... it looked like a nature fairy. Cool Fish!

I know Tibetans often study clouds to foretell happenings. OK, but how was this one created? Had I been calling up the nature fairies myself as I was so in tune with the land? Hmm ... I felt a small thrill of excitement.

Ooh, what wonders are we going to experience today?

I was sitting at the doorway of our tent watching everyone eat breakfast. My Human was pleased they'd run out of the dreaded yak-butter, but somehow everything seemed to smell of it anyway. There was an air of relaxation and contentment. Talk was of the giant mountain.

"Can't wait to speak out our peace messages again," said My Human. I looked at her lovingly as she glanced through the precious writings. It was so good to be with her and be part of the peace-work that was happening.

The Boyfriend pointed towards the distant peaks of the horizon. We could see dust dancing in the wind around a little cart that was making its way towards us. "Looks like we've got visitors," he said.

This was nothing unusual. Wherever we stopped the locals would appear as if from nowhere to come and investigate us. We did, of course, carry all sorts of modern gear, fascinating for those who live in such remote areas. As the cart came nearer we could see that it was drawn by two skinny little horses. The traces were decorated in typical style with bright blue squiggles and a gaily coloured flag which bobbed up and down with the horses' trotting motion over the rough stones of the dry ground. On board the cart was a family of nomads.

They tumbled out to greet us with "*Tashi Delek*" and the bringing of hands together. The faces of the adults were wizened and brown and their clothes covered in dirt, but still the women looked resplendent in their Tibetan *chupas* and striped aprons clasped with metal belts. The younger one wore red yak-skin boots and had her hair tied up with silver. They didn't seem at all shy and happily accepted an invitation to look around our camp.

In our tent the Boyfriend was demonstrating how clever the zips on his sleeping bags were to the amused gaze of what I thought must be the father, when a young boy, perhaps around seven years old, decided to pick me up.

I felt the tentativeness of someone not used to picking up penguins, but quite enjoyed his tickling of my tummy. He looked at My Human and said words, presumably translating as, "Please can I take him out to play?" She responded with a nod and a smile.

I was thrown into the air a few times not ungently – which was actually quite fun – and then plonked unceremoniously on the back of the cart. Before long the family had climbed up too and we were on the move – bump bump bump – as the little horses negotiated the larger rocks and the flag on its pole waved bright red and yellow in the beaming sunlight.

For a short while I enjoyed the adventure – just

for a very short while — until, looking around, I realised My Human wasn't on board the cart. Oy! Where is she? Oh, Flippin' Flippers! What was going on? Looking back at our camp I couldn't see any movement, just the tents receding slowly into the distance, until suddenly we went over a ridge. Then they weren't there anymore.

My Human would come and find me, no doubt.

But I was weighed down by a sort of numbness. Something was horribly wrong. Why wasn't she rushing up to collect me? The cart rumbled and bounced onwards and clouds of dust were now being thrown up behind us as if closing off what lay behind. With one particularly rough lurch I rolled over towards the edge of the cart in danger of being thrown off altogether. The boy picked me up and clung onto me. It was at this point that it dawned on me.

She wasn't going to come and collect me. The realisation hit me like a ton of flying fish in the face. She wasn't going to come and collect me. I knew what she would be thinking. That she had everything in life and this nomad family had nothing. That she couldn't just race after me and demand to have me back. The tradition of sharing and giving precious things to others was strong in Tibet. Real gifts were gifts from the heart. And I knew she would be thinking of the Tibetan teaching of impermanence – that all things move on. I knew she would be thinking that somehow, somehow she had to find a way to move on ... without me!!

I felt like I was falling through space.

I was on my own.

I screamed in my mind. *Help! I've been kidnapped! Help! I've been penguinnapped!*

But the little cart rumbled on. And the dust cloud billowed up, enveloping me in despair.

My nightmare fear of separation had been realised. Nothing worse could have happened. Surely this challenge was too big to find the treasure within.

I had been sure that through all my excellent character building and opening of my awareness I would be able to face fear like a true superhero, living fully in the moment, showing the bravado of being prepared to lose everything. Total commitment. But now that I had in fact lost everything I didn't feel like a superhero at all. It was as though the mask of who I thought I was had fallen away.

I feel naked and vulnerable. I have no protection.

I'm only a small fluffy penguin. I can't do strong anymore. Please! I need help ...

Penguins can't cry very well; shedding loads of tears means the eyes would freeze over in the cold of our ancestral home. Instead, our hearts break.

Bang!

Into a thousand pieces ...

Such was my jumbled haze of shock and fear I scarcely noticed that we had crossed a wide plain with beige tufts of grasses pushing through into this harsh world, strewn with grazing yak and sheep. We arrived at a large heavy brown yak-hair tent held down with rocks and the boy carried me inside.

It was dark and the air was filled with acrid smoke from a dung fire in the middle underneath a hole in the roof. An old woman was stirring a blackened pot on the fire. Beside her a young girl was struggling with a tall, thin butter churn below strings of dried meat.

To one side across a stash of pots there was a little wooden altar adorned with dishes and butter-lamps. The only other furniture was a large platform covered with carpets, skins and cushions. Curled up here was a tiny girl. She wore what appeared to be an old torn rag, but there were turquoise beads in her hair and her charcoal eyes shone with loveliness.

She jumped up on hearing her brother and toddled over to him with outstretched arms. I was placed into two little podgy hands and found myself looking up into a smile brimming with delight. She hugged me tightly and said something. I didn't have to guess what the words meant. It was obvious she was saying "Love you always".

A tiny flame lit in my heart.

In the days that followed, she barely let me out of her clasp.

If there's one thing I've learnt it's this; I can't avoid tough stuff and unexpected nasty happenings, but by facing these things I find treasure.

It was vital to trust in this process.

Gradually I adapted to the new circumstances that had been thrust upon me – that of a nomad existence on a high mountain plateau far away from all that I had known. Life was tough. Survival was the main object of every day. There was no one else to help the family. They relied totally on their own resources. But there was something in the simplicity of living in harmony with the rawness of the land that was very real. And the caring for each other gave everything meaning.

Piece by slow piece my heart was put back together, glued with the love of one tiny being.

But I couldn't forget My Human. The ache for her didn't go away. It was like a heavy ball of sadness that rolled about inside me. In particular I remembered how she'd say with a calm, understanding expression, "With love, there is no separation". Well, then. Were we not now separate?

Then one night as the chills of autumn were starting to bite, causing the Tiny One to hold me tighter still, I had a dream:

My Human is sitting in a cafe drinking tea, listening intently to a young maroon-robed monk. He is carrying a camera and wearing sunglasses on top of his head as though it's in no way strange to have a mix of the ancient and the modern. "I'm so excited that the Dalai Lama has given me his blessing to build a school for nomad children near my village. It'll overcome much of the poverty. It's my dearest wish."

"We will raise funds to help," My Human says. "Please, tell us your story."

The monk sits back in his chair and, just for a second, looks very pale. Then he takes a deep breath and begins: "Because of the invasion, three quarters of the people in our area where I was born lost their lives ... including two hundred monks who were lined up and shot in front of our village. My uncle was one of them."

My Human holds a hand in front of her mouth and gasps.

"My father," the monk continues, "was put in gaol for refusing to denounce the Dalai Lama and was beaten every day. My mother pleaded with the soldiers, so they beat her as well. She died from the wounds."

My Human stares silently, struggling to take in this horror.

"I was lucky," he goes on. "I joined a group and escaped over the mountains. And now I've been studying to be a monk for the last twelve years."

"But how do you feel about it? Surely you must be seething with hatred underneath?"

"No. That's not the Tibetan way. I have inner peace. For twelve years I haven't felt any anger in my heart."

There's a long silence. Then My Human ventures

quietly, almost to herself, "I think at last I understand ... that ... freedom is of our own choosing. And when we can reach this freedom, then we have found inner peace."

"Yes. You are the one who creates your own world. The way to change a situation is to master your own reaction to it."

I spent much of the following day pondering this dream.

I could see that my nomad family, in spite of having to tackle the great uncertainties of living within the earth's daily breath, the harsh winds and the sparseness of vegetation, seemed to accept with grace the cards that life dealt them and to appreciate each other and the gifts this brought them. Perhaps they did in fact have freedom.

But what about me? Pegbert inside my head is still insisting I'm being held captive. I shouldn't be here. I don't have freedom. That's not inner peace, is it? But what if I did let go my feelings of being hard done by? Would I too have freedom? Is it a choice I can make?

At least I have one big advantage now. I don't have to go in any more washing machines. I can be as grubby as I like!

And hadn't I just experienced a connection with My Human? I could tell she was OK; the dream had left me with a lovely feeling of closeness to her.

I longed for another one.

It was many weeks before another dream came, many weeks of accepting the simplicity and toughness of living in a small group in an isolated place. And then it arrived:

My Human is standing in front of a crowd. And showing pictures – of me!!! "He was a rock climber, an ice climber, a ski mountaineer, a pilgrim ... You name it, he'd done it ... a highly experienced member of our team."

Even mid-dream I could feel Pegbert puffing up with pride. Of course, such an important penguin ...

" ... so I had to let Yannick go. I was completely devastated ... But at least now we have an undercover agent in Tibet. And we eagerly await his reports."

I awoke feeling strangely satisfied. I hadn't been forgotten after all. My life still had great purpose.

The old woman was stirring up the embers of the fire and wafts of smoke were rousing the family to the morning routine. I could hear the long peeyooh call of a buzzard outside. The Tiny One hugged and snuggled me, looking down with such love that my heart nearly burst, this time with happiness.

Then it dawned on me. I'm doing my job after all. My job is to be cuddly. I was fine as I was at the beginning. But now I know why. It's because I'm giving joy. Giving joy is more important than any superhero task could ever be.

Life's great adventures will continue, but I finally know that my promise has been fulfilled.

Part of me deep inside has grown. I built a better me. And I discovered the treasure of Happiness.

Anyway, how many penguins do you know who are undercover agents in Tibet?

Shut up, Pegbert!